English Revision
Higher Level

Larry Cotter

GILL EDUCATION

Gill Education
Hume Avenue
Park West
Dublin 12
www.gilleducation.ie

Gill Education is an imprint of M.H. Gill & Co.

© Larry Cotter 2018

978 07171 80509

Design by Liz White Designs
Print origination by Carole Lynch

At the time of going to press, all web addresses were active and contained information
relevant to the topics in the book. Gill Education does not, however, accept responsibility
for the content or views contained on those websites. Content, views and addresses may
change beyond the publisher or author's control. Students should always be supervised
when reviewing websites.

For permission to reproduce photographs, the author and publisher gratefully
acknowledge the following:
© Alamy: 6, 15, 16, 29, 37T, 41, 44, 54TL, 69, 86, 114, 139; Courtesy of Bloomsbury:
97; Courtesy of Harrison's Fund: 67; © Irish Independent: 30; © iStock: 35, 37BR,
38, 54TR, 54B, 77, 81, 87, 119, 121, 126, 127, 134, 138, 141; © Shutterstock: 37BL;
Courtesy of Sony Ireland: 64.
The author and publisher have made every effort to trace all copyright holders,
but if any have been inadvertently overlooked we would be pleased to make the
necessary arrangement at the first opportunity.

The paper used in this book is made from the wood pulp of managed forests.
For every tree felled, at least one tree is planted, thereby renewing natural resources.

CONTENTS

Introduction

This book is a **practical guide** to Junior Cycle Higher Level English. It covers all areas of the course, focusing on **how** to **achieve high scores** in **each element** of **assessment**. It will help you to **prepare** for your assessment by:

- **Focusing** your revision on the 23 **Learning Outcomes** you have achieved in English.
- **Demonstrating** how to write excellent **sample answers** to exam questions.
- **Guiding** your **revision** of key elements of **fiction, drama, media, poetry** and **non-fiction prose**.
- **Explaining** a variety **of questions** you could face, and offering **clear hints** on how to approach them.
- **Dealing** with the **final assessment** as well as your **classroom-based assessments** and written task.

How to use this book

Read each section **carefully**. The **focus** of the section in the **title** relates to **key skills** you have developed during the course of your Junior Cycle. The **introduction** to each section explains this focus for you. In addition, you should closely examine the **aims** at the start of each section. They will help to remind you of the **purpose** of the **chapter** and how it relates to the **assessment**.

You will also notice that at various points in each unit you are given **text box reminders** to help reinforce important points:

1. **Exam Focus** – essential practical **advice** on **managing** your **performance** of key exam tasks.
2. **Key Point** – reminder of **crucial elements** in the key skills examined in Junior Cycle English.
3. **Learning Outcomes** – specific focus on tasks are related to the **23 outcomes** for assessment

Each section explains what is required by giving **worked sample questions**, **hints** and **answers**. You should **read** these several times to help you understand what you are expected to do for a particular type of question.

Finally, it's over to you to use the sample exam questions at the end of each chapter as a focus for **your own practice** as you attempt your own answers.

Learning Outcomes

There are 23 **Learning Outcomes** eligible for assessment as part of the Junior Cycle English **final written exam**. A number of other Learning Outcomes are assessed as part of the classroom-based assessments.

The chart below indicates some instances where the Learning Outcomes are explicitly addressed in this book. Learning Outcomes for final written assessment are indicated by a ⟹ L.O. **R 1**

LO	Text	Placement
R1	Read texts with fluency, understanding and competence, decoding groups of words/phrases and not just single words.	Chapter 2 Chapter 5 Chapter 6
R2	Read for a variety of purposes: learning, pleasure, research, comparison.	Chapter 3 Chapter 6 Chapter 7
R3	Use a wide range of reading comprehension strategies appropriate to texts, including digital texts: to retrieve information; to link to previous knowledge, follow a process or argument, summarise, link main ideas; to monitor their own understanding; to question, analyse, synthesise and evaluate.	Chapter 3 Chapter 4 Chapter 9
R4	Use an appropriate critical vocabulary while responding to literary texts.	Chapter 1 Chapter 2
R6	Read their texts for understanding and appreciation of character, setting, story and action: to explore how and why characters develop, and to recognise the importance of setting and plot structure.	Chapter 1 Chapter 6
R7	Select key moments from their texts and give thoughtful value judgements on the main character, a key scene, a favourite image from a film, a poem, a drama, a chapter, a media or web-based event.	Chapter 1 Chapter 4 Chapter 6
R8	Read their texts to understand and appreciate language enrichment by examining an author's choice of words, the use and effect of simple figurative language, vocabulary and language patterns, and images, as appropriate to the text.	Chapter 3 Chapter 4 Chapter 6 Chapter 7
R9	Identify, appreciate and compare the ways in which different literary, digital and visual genres and sub-genres shape texts and shape the reader's experience of them.	Chapter 2 Chapter 4 Chapter 7 Chapter 10
R11	Identify and comment on features of English at word and sentence level using appropriate terminology, showing how such features contribute to overall effect.	Chapter 3 Chapter 4 Chapter 10

LO	Text	Placement
R12	Understand how word choice, syntax, grammar and text structure may vary with context and purpose.	Chapter 4
R13	Appreciate a variety of registers and understand their use in the written context.	Chapter 3 Chapter 7
W1	Demonstrate their understanding that there is a clear purpose for all writing activities and be able to plan, draft, re-draft, and edit their own writing as appropriate.	Chapter 3 Chapter 8
W3	Write for a variety of purposes, for example to analyse, evaluate, imagine, explore, engage, amuse, narrate, inform, explain, argue, persuade, criticise, comment on what they have heard, viewed and read.	Chapter 1 Chapter 2 Chapter 5 Chapter 6 Chapter 7
W4	Write competently in a range of text forms, for example letter, report, multi-modal text, review, blog, using appropriate vocabulary, tone and a variety of styles to achieve a chosen purpose for different audiences.	Chapter 5 Chapter 9
W6	Use editing skills continuously during the writing process to enhance meaning and impact: select vocabulary, reorder words, phrases and clauses, correct punctuation and spelling, reorder paragraphs, remodel, manage content.	Chapter 9
W7	Respond imaginatively in writing to their texts, showing a critical appreciation of language, style and content, choice of words, language patterns, tone, images.	Chapter 1 Chapter 2 Chapter 5 Chapter 6 Chapter 7
W8	Write about the effectiveness of key moments from their texts, commenting on characters, key scenes, favourite images from a film, a poem, a drama, a chapter, a media or web-based event.	Chapter 6
W9	Engage in the writing process as a private, pleasurable and purposeful activity, and using a personal voice as their individual style is thoughtfully developed over the years.	Chapter 5
W10	Use and apply their knowledge of language structures, for example sentence structure, paragraphing, grammar, to make their writing a richer experience for themselves and the reader.	Chapter 2 Chapter 5 Chapter 6 Chapter 10
W11	Use language conventions appropriately, especially punctuation and spelling, to aid meaning and presentation and to enhance the reader's experienceuse language conventions appropriately, especially punctuation and spelling, to aid meaning and presentation, and to enhance the reader's experience.	Chapter 5 Chapter 9
W12	Demonstrate an understanding of how syntax, grammar, text structure and word choice may vary with context and purpose.	Chapter 4

LO	Text	Placement
O8	Listen actively in order to interpret meaning, compare, evaluate effectiveness of, and respond to drama, poetry, media broadcasts, digital media, noting key ideas, style, tone, content and overall impact in a systematic way.	Chapter 8
O12	Demonstrate how register, including grammar, text structure and word choice, varies with context and purpose in spoken texts.	Chapter 8

1 Making Sense of Drama: Shakespearean Drama

Appreciating character, setting, story and action

Storytelling has always fascinated us. From your favourite childhood bedtime fairytale to the latest Netflicks TV drama, the promise of a story well told will always be appealing. Over your three years in Junior Cycle English, you have explored stories in the form of novels, films, short stories and drama. Elements common to all forms of storytelling include:

Character	A person in a play, poem or story.
Setting	The time and place where a drama or story is set.
Story	A tale made up to entertain or amuse.
Action	The pattern of events in a plot.

In this section you will revise these **key ideas** by looking closely at **dramatic** storytelling. The **unseen** and **studied extracts** we will discuss here have one thing in common: they were all written by the master storyteller **William Shakespeare**. We will **outline** the **main elements** of all **drama** and show you how to discuss Shakespeare's plays using **suitable vocabulary** in the correct way.

exam focus

All students of Junior Cycle Higher Level English **MUST** study a **Shakespearean play**.

 L.O. R 4

Use an appropriate critical vocabulary while responding to literary texts.

In the exam, your knowledge of **drama** will be tested in different ways:

- **Reading an unseen extract** from the text of a play.
- Answering **short questions** on the script:
  - **matching** terms
  - **multiple-choice** questions
- **Composing a sentence or short paragraph** of your own.
- **Responding to pictures** in the form of still images of key moments in the play.
- **Writing** in **various styles** to display your **understanding** of the **story or characters**.
- **Applying** your **knowledge** of key ideas to the **play you studied** in class.
- **Developing** your **response** in **longer answers** on studied plays.

Areas to revise

Characters	Key people who change or develop over the course of a story or play.
Themes	Main ideas explored in the drama or story.
Conflict	Tension in a situation between characters in a drama or story.
Key scenes	Significant action in a particular place at a certain time.
Stagecraft	Areas or skills used to tell a story on stage, e.g. acting, props and lighting.
Personal response	Your own reaction to a key scene or character.

Characters

Most drama questions focus on the **people portrayed** on stage in the play. Read character questions carefully. <u>Underline</u> or <mark>highlight</mark> key words in the question.

Next, **pick out words** or **phrases** in the extract that tell you something useful about the **personality** of the character.

If a question focuses on **one** particular **character**, then you should pay attention to:

- **What** he or she **says**
- **What others** say **about them**
- The **actions** they **perform** while on stage.

The text in *italics* is referred to as **stage directions**. This gives us some idea of when movement or actions should happen. Sometimes the stage directions reveal how a character is feeling at a particular moment.

Remember to read both **dialogue** and **stage directions**. Both can reveal a lot about character.

 L.O. R 6

Read texts for understanding and appreciation of character, setting, story and action:

- to explore how and why characters develop
- to recognise the importance of setting and plot structure

Sample questions, answer and hints

Read the text below and the extract from Shakespeare's play, *Henry V.* Then answer the questions which follow.

Note: Underlined words are explained on the following page.

The background

King Henry has just ascended to the throne of England. During his youth, he spent some time in France where he enjoyed sport, dancing and going to parties. Now he has inherited the crown he must devote himself to serious issues. His political advisers have told him that he has a justifiable claim to the kingdom of France.

The characters

King Henry V – newly crowned English king

Exeter – Duke of Exeter, uncle to the king

Ambassador – messenger from the French prince

Dauphin – Prince of France and heir to the throne

In this scene, King Henry meets with an ambassador for the Dauphin, the eldest son of the French king and heir to the throne, according to French claims.

> **King Henry:** Call in the messengers sent from the <u>Dauphin</u>.
>
> *Exeunt some attendants*
>
> Now are we well resolv'd; and, by God's help
>
> And yours, the noble sinews of our power,
>
> France being ours, we'll bend it to our awe,
>
> Or break it all to pieces!
>
> *Enter ambassadors of France*
>
> Now are we well prepar'd to know the pleasure
>
> Of our fair cousin Dauphin.
>
> **Ambassador:** Your Highness, lately sending into France,
>
> Did claim some certain dukedoms in the right
>
> Of your great predecessor, King Edward the Third.
>
> In answer of which claim, the Prince our master
>
> Says that you savour too much of your youth,
>
> And bids you be advis'd there's nought in France
>
> That can be with a <u>nimble galliard</u> won;
>
> You cannot <u>revel</u> into dukedoms there.
>
> He therefore sends you, <u>meeter</u> for your spirit,
>
> This <u>tun</u> of treasure; and, in lieu of this,
>
> Desires you let the dukedoms that you claim
>
> Hear no more of you. This the Dauphin speaks.

King Henry: What treasure, uncle?

Exeter: Tennis-balls, my liege.

King Henry: We are glad the Dauphin is so pleasant with us;
His present and your pains we thank you for.
When we have match'd our rackets to these balls,
We will in France, by God's grace, play a set
Shall strike his father's crown into the <u>hazard</u>.
And we understand him well,
How he comes o'er us with our wilder days,
Not measuring what use we made of them.
But tell the Dauphin I will keep my state,
Be like a king, and show my sail of greatness,
When I do rouse me in my throne of France;
And tell the pleasant Prince this mock of his
Hath turn'd his balls to gun-stones, and his soul
Shall stand sore charged for the wasteful vengeance
That shall fly with them; for many a thousand widows
Shall this his mock mock of their dear husbands;
Mock mothers from their sons, mock castles down;
And some are yet ungotten and unborn
That shall have cause to curse the Dauphin's scorn.
So get you hence in peace; and tell the Dauphin
His jest will savour but of shallow wit,
When thousands weep more than did laugh at it.
Convey them with safe conduct. Fare you well.
Exeunt ambassadors

Dauphin: French prince

nimble galliard: lively dancing

revel: party

meeter: more suitable

tun: cask

hazard: danger or part of a tennis court, scores in tennis

Question 1

In the case of each of the following, write the letter corresponding to the correct answer in the appropriate box.

(a) As a young man in France, Henry spent time:
    A. Playing games and socialising
    B. Studying mathematics   **A.**
    C. Fighting duels

(b) The ambassador offers King Henry a present of:
    A. Precious jewels
    B. A box of tennis balls   **B.**
    C. The deeds to some land

(c) Which one of the following best describes Henry's tone in the lines:
    'We are glad the Dauphin is so pleasant with us;
    His present and your pains we thank you for.'
    A. Grateful
    B. Happy   **C.**
    C. Sarcastic

(d) Which one of the following is the best explanation of the lines:
    'some are yet ungotten and unborn
    That shall have cause to curse the Dauphin's scorn.'
    A. The Dauphin is angry because he didn't get what he wants.
    B. People who are not even born will live to regret the   **B.**
       Prince's disrespect.
    C. A wicked spell has been cast on the unborn children.

(e) Which one of the following is the best explanation of the lines:
    'Convey them with safe conduct.'
    A. Show them the way out.
    B. Escort them and protect them on their journey.   **B.**
    C. Make sure they behave themselves.

 L.O. W 3

Write for a variety of purposes, for example to:

* analyse
* evaluate
* imagine
* explore, etc.

Question 2   *20 marks*

Look carefully at this **still** image from a film adaptation of *Henry V*.

Based on your reading of the extract on the previous pages, **identify** and **explain two ways** in which this **image portrays** the **character of Henry**.

Allow 12 minutes for
20-mark questions.

Sample answer

This **image** portrays the **character** of Henry initially through the **setting** and **action**. It was taken outdoors in a rural situation but the location is no ordinary field, it is a **medieval battlefield**. The men on horseback carry **props** – they are **armed** with swords and carry **long shields** to protect themselves from attack. They are led by Henry whose threat to carry out 'wasteful vengeance' on the Dauphin and his subjects has obviously led to savage warfare. Henry **dominates** the centre of this image on his white charger and is literally shown **leading** his army into battle.

The photograph **illustrates** what Henry had in mind when he promised in his speech on pages 3–4 to:

> 'Be like a king, and show my sail of greatness,
> When I do rouse me in my throne of France.'

His **posture** with the sword held aloft in his right hand reflects the **aggression** expressed in his speech to the ambassador. Also, the image of a young king risking life and limb to fight in the **front line** expresses the **courage** of a character who is not afraid of conflict or intimidated by his enemies.

EXAMINER'S COMMENT

- Clear **focus** on how the **image** portrays **character**.
- Candidate analyses impact of setting, **action**, **props** and **posture**.
- Points supported with **evidence** from image and text.

MARKS AWARDED: Ex. 20/20 (90–100%) Distinction

- On **longer questions** you will be expected to write **several paragraphs**.
- **Highlight the key words** in the question and use them to **plan your answer**.
- Always use **quotation marks** for the **title of a play** and for **quotations** from the extract.
- The **key skill** here is to **explain, analyse and discuss**.
- **Demonstrate** your **appreciation** of **character, setting** and **story** by **explaining** clearly and concisely.
- **Focus** on the question and **always give reasons** to back up your ideas.

- Answer each question below with **several short paragraphs**.
- Use each paragraph to **develop one main idea** relevant to the question.
- **Read** the **hints** provided and use them to **practise** by writing an answer of your own.

Question 3   *20 marks*

King Henry is insulted by the message he receives from the Dauphin. Why is he so upset?

> ### Hints: Question 3
>
> - You are asked to **identify why** the king feels **insulted** by the Dauphin. The Dauphin has sent both a verbal message through his ambassador and a physical gift.
> - King Henry is **insulted by the words** of the Dauphin's, **and by the gift** of a 'tun' of tennis balls.
> - In your answer you should **pinpoint the precise words** which so **offended** King Henry. Your second paragraph will **link these words to the 'gift'** of the tennis balls. Look again at 'The background' paragraph for further **clues** as to why this **present combined with the words** of the message would have angered the new king at this time.
> - Finally, you should give some thought to the fact that the **Dauphin is a prince** while **Henry is a king**. The **difference between** their respective **ranks** is also relevant to this question.

Question 4   *20 marks*

If you were directing the actors in this scene, what advice would you give to the actor playing King Henry about how to deliver his speeches here?

> ### Hints: Question 4
>
> - Answering the second question requires you to have a good understanding of the **character of King Henry**. We know from the background information that he is a **new ruler** whose **reputation** from the playboy lifestyle of his youth

may be a source of **embarrassment** to him. The introduction also reveals a man **under some pressure** to claim authority over a 'foreign' land.

- His **initial lines**, directed to his court before the ambassador enters, are full of **resolute conviction** that either France will come under his control or he will destroy it. Advice to an actor should concentrate on **how these lines must be delivered**. Aspects of performance include **strength, tone** and **pace** of the **speaking voice, posture, facial expression** and **movement**.

- The second speech is much longer and a good answer will focus on **how the character develops** as the king becomes **more threatening**. Should the actor **remain in the same position**, or what **movements** would you recommend? For all directions given to the actor, you must **explain why** these are appropriate. Quote from the text of the play the words or lines that support your view.

Question 5   30 marks

Imagine the scene where the ambassador returns to France. Write the dialogue between the ambassador and his master, the Dauphin.

Allow 20 minutes for 30-mark questions.

Hints: Question 5

- The last question often carries more marks, as you are being asked to **write** a short piece **continuing the story**. Here your **ability** to **comprehend** the **dramatic situation** is being tested, along with the **skill** of **writing** a short piece of **dialogue**. If the instructions are open-ended, then **any style** of **dialogue** is acceptable.

- Do not feel that you are expected to continue the Elizabethan register of Shakespeare. A modern, **colloquial conversation** between the ambassador and his master would be suitable, as long as you **capture** the **difficulty faced** by the **ambassador**. He must **bring bad news** to the Dauphin and **diplomacy** would prevent him from telling the full truth.

- The scene you write will be short as you have very little time, but it could be either serious or comical in tone, and the only real restriction is that it should **include** at least the **characters** of the **ambassador** and the **Dauphin** formatted correctly as **dialogue**.

Suitable vocabulary

Learn the words below and study the **definitions**. You must use the **correct vocabulary** when commenting on drama.

The style of a good answer depends on using the **best language** in **appropriate** ways.

Catastrophe	The death of the hero or heroine in a drama.
Comedy	A story written to amuse the audience by highlighting the foolishness of people.

Conflict	The tension in a situation between characters in a drama.
Dialogue	Words spoken by characters in a poem, story or drama.
Hero/heroine	Central character in a story – usually a noble person who saves the day.
Irony	Contrast between what a character says and what is actually the case.
Mood	Feeling or state of mind created by a story or scene.
Plot	The pattern of events in a story.

Conflict

All drama relies on conflict to **generate** and **sustain** the **interest** of the audience. This conflict usually makes the audience feel **tension**. Dramatic scenes usually involve conflict like the clash between King Henry and the French ambassador in the extract on pages 3–4.

Sometimes, however, the **conflict** is not simply between two opposing individuals or groups but **within the mind** of a single person. The following exam question illustrates this well, as there are a number of ways in which the struggle between opposites is dramatised here.

Sample question and answer

Read the extract below from *Much Ado About Nothing* by William Shakespeare. Answer the question which follows.

The background
The Prince of Aragon (Don Pedro) and his soldiers return victorious from war and visit the house of Leonato, Governor of Messina. There, Leonato's daughter Hero is wooed by the prince's friend Claudio and their wedding is planned. Due to a wicked plot by the villain Don John, Claudio calls off the wedding at the last minute.

The characters
Beatrice – friend to Hero

Claudio – nobleman

Benedick – gentleman and best friend of Claudio

Hero – noble daughter of Leonato

Benedick and Beatrice are discussing Count Claudio and Hero, Claudio's bride to be. Mistakenly, Count Claudio thinks that Hero has been unfaithful to him and cancels their wedding. Beatrice weeps for her cousin Hero who, she strongly believes, has been wronged.

Exeunt (all but Benedick and Beatrice)

Benedick: (*With great kindness*) Lady Beatrice, have you wept all this while?

Beatrice: Yea, and I will weep a while longer.

Benedick: I will not desire that.

Beatrice: You have no reason. I do it freely.

Benedick: Surely I do believe your fair cousin is wronged.

Beatrice: Ah, how much might the man deserve of me that would right her!

Benedick: Is there any way to show such friendship?

Beatrice: A very even way, but no such friend.

Benedick: May a man do it?

Beatrice: It is a man's office, but not yours.

Benedick: I do love nothing in the world so well as you. Is not that strange?

Beatrice: As strange as the thing I know not. It were as possible for me to say I loved nothing so well as you. But believe me not; and yet I lie not. I confess nothing, nor I deny nothing. I am sorry for my cousin.

Benedick: By my sword, Beatrice, thou lovest me.

Beatrice: Do not swear, and eat it.

Benedick: I will swear by it that you love me, and I will make him eat it that says I love not you.

Beatrice: Will you not eat your word?

Benedick: With no sauce that can be devised to it. I protest I love thee.

Beatrice: Why then, God forgive me!

Benedick: What offence, sweet Beatrice?

Beatrice: You have stayed me in a happy hour. I was about to protest I loved you.

Benedick: And do it with all thy heart.

Beatrice: I love you with so much of my heart that none is left to protest.

Benedick: Come, bid me do anything for thee.

Beatrice: (*Pause*) ... Kill Claudio ...

Question 1   *25 marks*

Show how the conflict in this scene builds to a climactic moment.

 L.O. W 7

Respond imaginatively in writing to texts, showing a critical appreciation of:

- language
- style and content
- choice of words
- language patterns
- tone
- images

Allow 15 minutes for 25-mark questions.

Sample answer

The first sign of **tension** is that Beatrice has been **crying**. We know this because Benedick asks, 'Lady Beatrice, have you wept all this while?' She also tells him that she will continue crying 'a while longer'. There is **conflict** because he wants her to stop crying and his **tone** is very **sympathetic** to her friend but Beatrice is still upset.

Always **support** your points with **evidence** from the text, **dialogue** or **stage directions**.

The second area of conflict is that Benedick loves **Beatrice** and wants to prove that love but she **will not declare her love** for him. Beatrice replies to Benedick's declaration of love saying, 'I confess nothing, nor I deny nothing.' This must have been **tantalising** for Benedick as if she was teasing him by answering his question saying, 'No comment.'

The **conflict** seems to be over when Beatrice claims 'I love you with so much of my heart that none is left to protest.' Now the **two characters** on stage **agree** that their feelings for one another are mutual. It looks like the scene has reached a happy ending. Unfortunately, Benedick is so delighted that he offers to grant whatever Beatrice wishes him to do. Her reply introduces a **new kind of conflict**. When she asks Benedick to 'Kill Claudio' the conflict changes as we now have **two competing loyalties**. Benedick must **choose** between being **loyal to his best friend** or **killing that friend** to please his new lover.

Themes

Many of Shakespeare's plays deal with several **key ideas**. These themes are **introduced early** in the drama and **developed** as the story unfolds before our eyes. Whether you are writing about an **unseen extract** or a moment from **a play you have studied**, it is important to understand what is happening and how it relates to the main ideas in a story. Avoid simplistic labels when discussing important topics explored in a play. For example, instead of a one-word definition of the 'love' theme in *Romeo and Juliet* you should compose a **short phrase** like 'the struggle of young people to find true love'.

When you are **revising key themes** you will have **at least two**. You you must learn at least **ten key lines** from the play that are **relevant to that theme**. Another theme you could explore in *Romeo and Juliet* is 'the violent consequences of a bitter family feud'. This phrase tells the examiner a great deal more than a single-word expression of the theme of 'death'.

Glossary of key terms

Satire	A story or drama aiming to make a person or group of people appear ridiculous.
Scene	All the action taking place in a particular place at a particular time.
Soliloquy	When a character delivers his/her own thoughts as if to himself or herself.
Stage directions	Instructions giving information about props, the set and actors' movements.
Subplot	Secondary sequence of events in a play, usually involving minor characters.
Theme	Key idea explored in a poem, story or play.
Tragedy	Serious drama involving a crisis and resulting in an unhappy ending.
Villain	The principal evil character in a story.

> **exam focus**
>
> Learn each of these **key terms** and **definitions** and use them with confidence in your answers.

Key scenes

Writing about an unseen moment from a Shakespeare play is often followed up with a question where you are asked to discuss a **key scene** from the play that you have studied. This will require you to **identify** the **scene** and **explain** the impact it made on you by **discussing what makes it dramatic**. You should prepare at least three key moments from the play you have studied.

> **key point**
>
> It is essential to think about **how you feel** as you watch these moments on stage or film.

You must learn at least **five important lines** from each of the scenes below to **quote** as evidence to support your answer:

- Opening scene
- Climactic scene
- Final scene
- Your favourite scene

Your personal response to key moments will make your answer original and gain you higher marks.

> 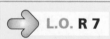 **L.O. R 7**
>
> Select key moments from texts and give thoughtful value judgements on:
> - the main character
> - a key scene
> - a favourite image from a film, a poem, etc.

Sample question, hints and answer
Question 1   *40 marks*
1. Name a play you have studied: *Romeo and Juliet*
2. Name the playwright: *William Shakespeare*
3. Choose a scene from this play you found either happy or sad. Describe how the playwright conveys this happiness or sadness.

25

Allow 25 minutes for 40-mark questions.

Hints

- **Choose** a scene from a play you have **studied well**, discussing your **personal response**.
- Select a **key moment**, identifying **aspects of the plot** that **prompted** your reaction.
- Provide **evidence** of at least one **dramatic device** or aspect of **performance** to improve your mark.
- Write in the **first person** ('I') to underline the fact that this is your own **personal response**.
- **Explain clearly** why the scene **produced feelings** of happiness or sadness.
- **Specific reference** to or quotation from the play is **essential.**

Sample answer

My favourite scene from *Romeo and Juliet* by William Shakespeare is Act II, scene 2. This scene takes place in Juliet Capulet's garden at night-time after the feast where the 'star crossed lovers' meet for the very first time. I enjoyed this scene above all others because it is the happiest scene in the play, in my opinion the hero and heroine are never quite as happy at any other point in the story.

It begins in a comical way, as Juliet is high on a balcony while Romeo is beneath her in the garden hidden from her view. Romeo is happy because he has fallen in love, again! Seeing his new love appear lit up in the window, he joyfully declares that 'Juliet is the sun'. This happy metaphor is just the first of many beautiful images in this scene. I really like the lines he says when he sees her leaning out, resting her cheek on her hand,

> 'O that I were a glove upon that hand,
> That I might touch that cheek!'

This is a very intimate and pleasant wish and we enjoy hearing him express it because we know his wish will be granted when he embraces her later.

It is a happy scene because Juliet's wish also comes true in this scene. Unaware of the fact that she is being spied on by Romeo, she wistfully regrets that a mere name divides them from each other. Referring to Romeo as a beautiful flower she insists that 'that which we call a rose by any other word would smell as sweet'. The fact that she is unhappy thinking they will never be lovers adds to the eventual happiness of the scene since we know Romeo is about to appear and declare his love.

All the barriers between them, as members of the feuding Montague and Capulet clans, are overcome when he bravely scales the wall and climbs up to kiss her. In this scene the ridiculous proposal of marriage is a happy antidote to the vicious antagonism of the 'ancient grudge' the families bear for one another. When Romeo begs her 'Wilt thou leave me so unsatisfied?', the audience shares in his delicious joy that she accepts him and the impossible dream comes true as they are engaged in spite of all the obstacles to their love.

Shakespeare realistically mixes happiness with sadness at the end of this scene because the lovers must say goodbye. Juliet expresses this perfectly when she tells him that 'parting is such sweet sorrow'. Even though he must leave we are happy in the knowledge that she will be reunited with him soon.

EXAMINER'S COMMENT

Indicators of quality:

- Initial sentence clearly identifies 'My favourite scene ...' **focusing on personal response**.
- **Detailed analysis** of **reasons why** the scene is **effective**
- Answer is **well shaped, developed and structured**

MARKS AWARDED: **Ex. 40/38 (90–100%)** Distinction

Stagecraft

A question about a **character** may also ask you to make suggestions about how he or she should **appear on stage**. Look closely at the **dialogue** for clues about how the character is dressed in order to recommend an appropriate **costume**. Some characters may require special **make-up** to exaggerate certain aspects of their physical appearance. If **props** are mentioned, you should refer to them and how the character carries and uses the props.

Emotion can be dramatised by the actor's **facial expression** and physical **posture**. As well as using their body to communicate emotion, an actor's **tone of voice** is a key element of their craft. Directors must also instruct actors on when and how to use **silence** for dramatic effect.

Focused **knowledge** of **stagecraft** will earn you high marks in the exam.

Several elements can combine to create a mood on stage. **Lighting** is the most influential method of establishing atmosphere. **Music** can be used to suggest a change in mood or the passage of time. **Sound effects**, on the other hand, are often employed to make a scene sound more realistic.

More key terms

Costume	How an actor's clothing on stage or screen reveals aspects of character.
Facial expression	Emotion is expressed by the look on an actor's face, exaggerated in mime.
Lighting	Mood and atmosphere is created and changed by adjusting the light.
Make-up	Cosmetics are used to highlight aspects of a character's key features.
Movement	Actors physically communicate their characters and aspects of the plot.
Posture	Body language can tell us a lot about a character's frame of mind.
Props	Physical objects carried by actors for a purpose suggested by the script.
Sound effects	Recorded noises used to give a realistic quality to the action on stage.
Soundtrack	On film or stage, music creates intense feeling.
Tone of voice	The way we speak articulates feeling more than the meaning of the words.

Personal response

Technical information and learning quotations by heart is not enough for full marks in a question about drama. Your most important skill is to **observe your own response** to words, lines and scenes. **Notice how you feel** about the main **characters** and write notes explaining what precisely causes you to feel the way you do about them.

The following questions will help you to think about your response to characters.

Hero/heroine

- **Who** are the characters you **admire**?
- **Why** do you have a lot of **respect** for him/her?
- **How** do they **deal** with problems?
- Choose a **scene** where he/she is **heroic**.
- **How** does his/her character **change**?

Olivia Hussey as Juliet

Villain

- **Who** is the **most evil** person in the drama?
- **How** do they **cause suffering**?
- **Describe** their **relationship** to the hero/heroine.
- **What** do you **admire** about him/her?
- **Why** is he/she **important** to the story?

To wrap up this section, you can practise your skills and appreciation of drama by attempting this question.

Al Pacino as Shylock

Exam Question 2017 (Junior Cycle 2017, Final Examination, English Higher Level)

Section C – Appreciating Character, Setting, Story and Action
Read the text printed below and the extract from Shakespeare's play, *The Tempest*. Answer the questions which follow.

The background
Prospero, Duke of Milan, was expelled from his Dukedom by his brother Antonio. He finds refuge on an island. Prospero has magical powers that allow him to control spirits, humans and the elements. An opportunity presents itself for Prospero to get revenge, when Antonio arrives on the same island. Antonio is in the company of Alonso, the King of Naples.

The characters
Alonso – King of Naples

Ferdinand – King Alonso's son

Sebastian – King Alonso's brother

Antonio – Prospero's scheming brother

Gonzalo – an honest old courtier

Prospero – former Duke of Milan (a magician)

exam focus

There are **75 marks** available for this section. **Timing** is crucial. You should spend **45 minutes** answering this question.

As the extract opens, Alonso and his companions are searching the island for Ferdinand, who is missing. Antonio and Sebastian are plotting to kill Alonso. Prospero controls events from above. The audience can see Prospero but the other characters on stage cannot see him. Magically, Prospero makes a procession of spirits appear. They bring a banquet of food. Dancing around a table, they invite the weary travellers to eat. Just as the travellers attempt to taste the food, Prospero makes the banquet disappear.

Enter Alonso, Sebastian, Antonio, Gonzalo and others.

Gonzalo: I can go no further, sir;
My old bones ache; here's a maze trod indeed
Through meandering paths! By your patience,
I needs must rest me.

Alonso: Old lord, I cannot blame thee,
Who am myself seized with weariness,
Sit down and rest.
Even here I will put off my hope, and keep it
No longer: Ferdinand is dead
Whom thus we stray to find, and nature mocks   10
Our frustrated search on this island. Well, let him go.

Antonio: *[To Sebastian]* I am right glad that he's so out of hope.
Do not, for one repulse, forgo the purpose
That you resolved to effect.*

Sebastian: *[To Antonio]* The next advantage we will take thoroughly.

Antonio: *[To Sebastian]* Let it be to-night
For, now they are oppressed with travel, they
Will not, nor cannot, use such vigilance
As when they are fresh.

Sebastian: *[To Antonio]* I say to-night: no more.   20

*Solemn and strange music; enter Prospero above, invisible to the other
characters. Enter several strange Spirits, bringing in a banquet; they dance
about it with gentle actions of salutation, inviting Alonso, etc., to eat.*

Alonso: What harmony is this? My good friends, hark!

Gonzalo: Marvellous sweet music!

Alonso: Give us kind keepers, heavens! What were these?

Gonzalo. If in Naples
I should report this now, would they believe me?
Who, though they are of monstrous shape, yet
Their manners are more gentle-kind, you shall find,
Than many of our human generation.

The strange Spirits depart.

Prospero: *[Aside]* Honest lord,
Thou hast said well; for some of you there present   30
Are worse than devils.

Alonso: I cannot too much muse
Such shapes, such gesture, and such sound, expressing
(Although they want the use of tongue) a kind
Of excellent dumb discourse.

Prospero: *[Aside]* Keep your praise till the end.

Antonio: They vanish'd strangely.

Sebastian: No matter, since
They have left the banquet behind; for we have stomachs –
Will't please you taste of what is here?   40

Alonso: Not I.

Gonzalo: Faith sir, you need not fear. When we were boys,
Who would believe that there were such creatures,
Dew-lapp'd like bulls, whose throats had hanging at 'em
Wallets of flesh? Yet now we find
Explorers bring us proof of.

Alonso: I will stand to, and feed.

Thunder and lightning. As if by magic, the banquet vanishes.

*to kill Alonso

Question 1   *10 marks*

In the case of each of the following, write the letter corresponding to the correct answer in the appropriate box.

(a) Which word best describes Alonso's mood at the start of the extract?
(Lines 5–11)

    A. Relieved

    B. Aggressive

    C. Disconsolate

(b) Based on what you have read in the text and the extract above, which of the following characters are both villains?

    A. Alonso and Gonzalo

    B. Gonzalo and Antonio

    C. Antonio and Sebastian

(c) Which one of the following is the best explanation of the lines:
'... they are oppressed with travel, they
Will not, nor cannot, use such vigilance
As when they are fresh. (Lines 17–19)?'

    A. They are anxious to continue their journey.

    B. They are so tired that they can be easily caught offguard.

    C. With the Spirits' help they are now prepared for anything.

(d) Which one of the following is the best explanation of the lines:
'I cannot too much muse
Such shapes, such gesture, and such sound, expressing
(Although they want the use of tongue) a kind
Of excellent dumb discourse. (Lines 32–35)?'

    A. It's remarkable how these forms can say so much without the use of speech.

    B. I don't want to think about what I have just seen.

    C. I do not understand what these creatures mean at all.

(e) Asides are used by Prospero in this extract. What is an aside?

A. A position for an actor on the extreme left or right of the stage.

B. Thoughts spoken out loud, largely for the benefit of the audience.

C. A group of characters who comment on the action in a drama.

Question 2   20 marks

The magical world depicted in *The Tempest* creates opportunities for a director to stage the play in an imaginative way.

Based on your reading of the extract from *The Tempest* (pages 16–18), explain two things a director could do to stage this extract from the play in an imaginative way.

Question 3   5 marks

Select one character from a Shakespearean play you have studied and list five adjectives that identify this character's essential qualities.

Question 4   20 marks

Choose one of the qualities identified in your list above. Explain how at least two key moments from the play highlight this quality in your chosen character. Use your knowledge of the play to justify your viewpoints.

Question 5   20 marks

A film version is being made of the Shakespearean play you have studied. What would you include on a poster advertising the film to represent what you think is important in the play, and to create a sense of anticipation for its upcoming release? Explain your decisions with reference to the play.

2 Reading Speeches, Posters & Films: Appreciating Audience and Register

Every effort we make to **communicate** is aimed at the person or group of people we hope will hear the **message.** A distressed pilot sends out a 'Mayday' signal expecting air traffic controllers to be **listening** in. A roadside **advertisement** for insurance **targets** the **attention** of motorists. Coverage of an international soccer match is **broadcast** to football fans who didn't manage to get a ticket to the game. In each one of the examples above someone is trying to reach an **audience**.

When we think about sending any message, the first question we face is, 'What do I want to say?'

Next we must consider, 'Who do I want to hear it?' The **words** I choose will depend on how I answer both questions. **Register** is using the best words to reach a specific individual or group of people.

Purpose = what you are asked to write.
Audience = who you are writing to.
Register = how you express your ideas.

 **L.O. W 7**

Respond imaginatively in writing to texts, showing a critical appreciation of:

- language
- style and content
- choice of words
- language patterns
- tone
- images

The audience is the individual or social group you try to connect with. The words you use depend on your relationship to them.

The following exercise demonstrates the importance of using the **right words** with the **right people**.

Imagine you are answering a variety of phone calls from different people. Match the caller in the left-hand column with a suitable greeting from the list on the right. The first one is done for you.

Caller	Greeting
Best friend	Good morning. How can I help you?
Complete stranger	Hello. Who's speaking please?
Customer	Hi! How's it going?

In the exam, your awareness of **audience** and **register** can be tested in different ways:

- Reading an **unseen speech** to follow the **argument** being made.
- Answering **short questions** identifying **techniques** of **persuasion**.
- **Composing** a **speech** based on a successful example or **model**.
- **Writing** a critical **analysis** of media, e.g. an advert, photo or blog.
- **Designing** or writing an **advertisement** for a new product.
- **Identifying** key elements of good **descriptive writing**.

Areas to revise

Speech writing	Strategies aimed at convincing an audience.
Mass media	The variety of ways of reaching a target group.
Description	Capturing a character, scene or atmosphere through detail.
Features of quality	Essential aspects of the best descriptive writing.

Speech writing

The ancient skill of using a **carefully crafted speech** to **influence** the **opinions** of the public continues to shape our world. Modern political **speeches** may appear on **social media** or **television**, but the **methods** used to win the hearts of the **audience** are timeless.

A successful speech delivers a **clear message** to a specific **target group** using the best words to **convince** that audience. The **audience** could be anybody: from **adults** deciding how to cast a vote, **sports players** about to take to the pitch or **students** on their first day at a new school. A speech must take account of the **age** of the listeners, **what unites them** as a group and how they already **feel** about the **topic**.

When reading an unseen speech, ask yourself the following questions:

1. **Who** is **delivering** the speech?
2. What is the speaker's **purpose** or aim?
3. How does the **vocabulary** reflect the **audience** being spoken to?
4. What **patterns** do you notice in the speaker's **language**?
5. **How** does the speech put **images** before the audience in the form of **examples**?
6. In what way are the **feelings** of the audience being **changed** or **emphasised**?

This strategy is used in the sample question and answer below. Read the speech and the analysis that follows.

Suitable vocabulary

In the sample answer, **key terms** are used to explain methods of persuasion. **Learn** the words below and revise the **definitions**. You must use **appropriate** technical **language** when commenting on a speech.

> **exam focus**
>
> Learn key terms and definitions to use them correctly in your answers.

Antithesis	When two opposite ideas are put together to create a contrast.
Emotive language	Words used to elicit a powerful emotional feeling in the reader.
Imperative verbs	Verbs used as commands to convey urgency.
Slogans	Memorable short phrases that are often repeated.
Colloquial language	Informal language close to the style of everyday speech.
Hyperbole	Exaggeration for the sake of emphasis.

Sample questions, hints and answers

'The Man' from *School of Rock*

The background

In the film *School of Rock*, Dewey Finn, a struggling musician, accepts a job as a substitute teacher even though he has no previous experience of teaching.

> **GO ONLINE**
>
> Watch 'The Man – The School of Rock' (from 0:38–1:34) on YouTube or DVD.

On his first day at work he is hungover and tired but the students are waiting for class to begin. In the speech below, Dewey responds to the eager school children's request for him to teach them.

> You want me to teach you something?
> You want to learn something?
> Here's a useful lesson for you.
> Give up, just quit,
> because in this life, you can't win.

Yeah, you can try, but in the end you're just gonna lose, big time,
because the world is run by the Man.
The Man, oh, you don't know the Man.

He's everywhere.
In the White House …
down the hall …
Miss Mullins, she's the Man.
And the Man ruined the ozone,
he's burning down the Amazon,
and he kidnapped Shamu and put her in a chlorine tank!

And there used to be a way to stick it to the Man.
It was called rock 'n roll,
but guess what,
oh no, the Man ruined that, too,
with a little thing called MTV!

So don't waste your time
trying to make anything cool or pure or awesome
'cause the Man is just gonna call you a fat washed-up loser
and crush your soul.

So do yourselves a favour and just GIVE UP!

Question 1   15 marks

What reasons does Dewey put forward for just quitting?

Hint: Reason 1

Dewey tells the children that they can try to learn but they
will fail because of 'the Man'. There is no point in even
trying to succeed because 'the Man is everywhere'.
Powerful people like the president in the 'White House'
and 'Miss Mullins', the school principal, are mentioned as examples.

Allow 10 minutes for
15-mark questions.

Hint: Reason 2

The second reason he gives for quitting is
that there is no longer any way to resist
'the Man'. He tells them that there used to
be a way called 'rock 'n roll' but it was
'ruined' by 'MTV'.

 L.O. W 10

Use and apply knowledge
of language structures,
for example:

- sentence structure
- paragraphing
- grammar

to make writing a richer
experience.

Hint: Reason 3

Finally he claims that they are doomed to
fail and that they will suffer as a result.
They might try to create something 'cool
or pure or awesome' but stronger people
will humiliate them and 'crush' their souls.

Question 2 *20 marks*

Find evidence of four different features typically used in a good speech.

Allow 12 minutes for 20-mark questions.

Hint: Feature 1

Dewey uses **antithesis** to create a **contrast** between **winning** and **losing**. It has an impact because in the speech Dewey **compares success** and **failure** in stark language. He tells the students to 'quit'; that they're bound to 'lose'. On the other hand the 'world is run by the Man' who in **contrast** is powerful and successful. The 'Man' is 'everywhere' and the students 'can't win'.

Hint: Feature 2

Dewey uses **imperative verbs** as **commands** at the **start** and at the **end** of his speech. They have an impact because when he tells the children to 'Give up' it seems as if they have no choice and must accept defeat. His **instruction** to the children to 'just quit' is also like an order they must obey. He finishes his speech by repeating the same verb in the most **forceful way**, 'just GIVE UP!'

Hint: Feature 3

Colloquial language is used throughout this speech when Dewey says words like, 'quit', 'gonna', 'stick it' and 'awesome'. It has an impact because this **casual** and **simple vocabulary** is suitable for the young children who make up the **audience**. When he tells them that 'in the end' they're 'gonna lose big time' he is making sure that they understand his message because this vocabulary is commonly used and easily understood. It is the best **register** for his **message** to this **audience**.

Hint: Feature 4

There are **two slogans** used in the speech 'Give up, just quit' and 'just GIVE UP'. They have an impact because the two phrases are **short** and **memorable**. The words are **easy** to understand and the slogans **repeat** the same simple idea. He even combines the words from the first slogan in a more **catchy sentence** the second time when tells them to 'Just GIVE UP.'

Question 3 *15 marks*

Would you agree that the tone of Dewey Finn's speech to the school children is both pessimistic and cynical?

Sample answer

I agree that the **tone** of Dewey's speech is extremely **negative**. The lesson he sets out to teach them is **pessimistic** from the start. He tells the pupils to 'quit' because they 'can't win'.

Allow 10 minutes for 15-mark questions.

His **advice** is that there is no point in trying to succeed because they're 'just gonna lose, big time'. This pessimism continues when he explains that **hope** for happiness is **futile** because 'the Man ... is everywhere'. Dewey's belief is that the children are **guaranteed to fail** in life based on his own anger and disappointment. We know he is influenced by his own negative experiences when he says that 'the Man is gonna call you a fat washed up loser.' Based on these unhappy memories, Dewey predicts crushing defeat for his students.

More techniques of persuasion

The following **six methods** are also common ways of **convincing** an audience to accept a message. **Learn** the terms and **definitions**. Each one is also used in the longer sample answer to the question below.

The **skill** is to write in a **style suitable** for your **audience** and for the **occasion**.

Illustrate	Give clear examples as evidence to prove a point.
Parallelism	Repetition of words in a sentence to give balance or symmetry.
Register	Style of language suitable in a particular social situation.
Repetition	Words or phrases are used repeatedly.
Rhetorical question	A question that does not require an answer.
Tone	The reflection of the writer's attitude or feeling.

Question 4   40 marks

Imagine you were a **pupil** in this class. **Write** the **speech** you would give in **reply** to Dewey Finn. Use at least **three** of the **techniques** of persuasion outlined above.

Allow 25 minutes for 40-mark questions.

Sample answer

You want to just give up?
You want to throw away all our good work?
Here's what I think of your losing attitude.

Never give up, never quit.
If you believe in yourself,
If you have courage and faith,
then you will win, my friends.

You may lose heart,
You might feel like surrendering to panic and doubt.
Why should we allow the fearful voices to defeat our dreams?
Hope put Obama in the White House,

Hope won the Super Bowl for the New England Patriots,
Hope made Adele the Queen of the Grammys.

Take heart from the courage of famous winners:
Barcelona claiming victory over PSG against unbelievable odds,
One Direction achieving global success after finishing third in 'The X Factor',
J.K. Rowling's first novel was rejected twelve times
Her books have since earned her over £2 billion
more than any other writer.

Now why would you throw in the towel when the finishing line is in sight?

Believe in yourself.
Cherish your dreams.
Hold on to Hope.
Never give up and your dreams will come true.

EXAMINER'S COMMENT

- In this answer the candidate is successful because the speech fulfils all the **key terms** of the question. First, the speech is obviously written in reply to Dewey Finn's address to the class. The **content**, **structure** and **language** reflect Dewey's speech and use it as a model for the response. This answer begins with **two rhetorical questions**, 'You want to just give up? and 'You want to throw away all our good work?' These are highly effective **focusing comments** and **mimic** the opening lines of the original 'the Man' speech.

- Second, in common with all good speeches the answer includes many **examples** of **repetition**. The most effective example is when **three** sentences all **begin** in an **identical** way with the word 'Hope'. Using the same way to start each line helps to hammer home the point that it is vital to remain positive.

- The third important way this answer meets the requirements of the task is through clear use of **good examples** to **illustrate a point**. **Three** different stories of success are mentioned: 'Barack Obama', the 'New England Patriots' and the singer 'Adele'. In addition, three examples are given of unexpected success in the case of 'One Direction', 'Barcelona' and 'J.K. Rowling'. Using **specific well-known** examples helps to illustrate the idea by giving the reader a **familiar image** to **support** the key point.

MARKS AWARDED: Ex. 40/40 (90–100%) Distinction

 L.O. W 10

Use and apply knowledge of language structures, for example:
- sentence structure
- paragraphing
- grammar

to make writing a richer experience.

Question 5   25 marks

Give the title and author of a text on your course where one character gives advice to another person who has a problem. Describe the relationship, outline the nature of the problem and discuss the advice given in order to solve it.

(15)

Allow 15 minutes for 25-mark questions.

Title: *Romeo and Juliet*

Author: *William Shakespeare*

Sample answer

Relationship: From early in the play we see Romeo turning to Friar Laurence for support. The friar is Romeo's **counsellor** who has patiently listened to the story of his heartbreak over 'Rosaline'. Later when Romeo wishes to marry Juliet in secret, the friar **grants his wish**, hoping that the marriage will 'turn your households' rancour to pure love'.

Problem: At a crucial point in the plot, the hero Romeo faces a serious problem when he is **'banished'** from **Verona**. The Prince orders Romeo to go into **exile** as a **punishment** for the killing of Tybalt. He must leave 'in haste. Else, when he is found, that hour is his last.' Unknown to the Prince and the two families, Romeo is now married to Juliet and banishment would mean **separation** for the newlywed couple. In desperation, Romeo turns to Friar Laurence, convinced that **suicide** is his only option.

Advice: Laurence's response is a magnificent speech. He begins with a **rhetorical question** 'Art thou a man?' This strong **challenge** is aimed at bringing Romeo to his senses. He goes on to **give reasons** Romeo has to be grateful for his situation: 'Thy Juliet is alive', 'Tybalt would kill thee but thou slowest Tybalt' and 'the law that threatened death becomes thy friend and turns it to exile'. Each one of these is an **example** to Romeo of his good fortune. Friar Laurence is giving examples to **illustrate** his point that Romeo should be grateful to be alive.

The Friar also uses **repetition** very effectively to force home his point by following each one of the examples above with the refrain 'There are thou happy.' His message is expressed in a **metaphor** that serves as a catchy **slogan** for Romeo. Laurence compares him to a beast who is carrying a load which is light and easy, telling the distressed hero that 'a pack of blessings light upon thy back'. In this way a situation that seemed hopeless is transformed by a clever speech where Romeo is forced to count his blessings.

 L.O. W 12

Demonstrate an understanding of how syntax, grammar, text structure and word choice may vary with context and purpose.

Media

Every branch of the mass **media** aims to **communicate** a message to an **audience** using a suitable **register**. In your exam you could be given a photo, advertisement, newspaper article or web page and asked to **explain how** it **transmits** a message to the **viewer**. The key skills are:

- Observation – **noticing** all the elements in the text and how they fit together.
- Description – using **precise** vocabulary to create an **accurate image** of key elements.
- Analysis – **commenting** on **how** a text works and what makes it successful.
- Illustration – **giving examples** to **support** the points you make.
- Explanation – offering **clear reasons** to back up your ideas and opinions.

Suitable vocabulary

The grid below contains a sample of **technical terms** useful for analysis of several types of media. **Learn** these **definitions** and use them to **interpret** texts. A **sample question** and **model answer** are outlined here for you to use as a guideline.

Colour	This is used in drama and artwork to create mood or atmosphere.
Costumes	Clothing worn to create a fictional character on stage and in film.
Graphic	Images used in advertising to illustrate a product or setting.
Font	The style of lettering used in a document or poster.
Props	Physical objects carried by actors for a purpose suggested by the script in a drama, film or poster.
Tagline	A short line used in an advert that captures the essence of a film.

Sample question and answer

Question 1   15 marks
Is the movie **poster** on the following page an **effective** way to **advertise** the film and DVD of *School of Rock*? **Explain** your answer using **evidence** from the poster to **support** your points.

Allow 10 minutes for 15-mark questions.

Sample answer
The poster is highly effective because it is dominated by a **striking graphic** of the central **character** from the film. The actor Jack Black strikes a typical rock-star **pose**, and the electric guitar **prop** suggests that this *fictional character* is a musician. His **costume** of trousers, jacket and tie **contrast** with the prop but link well to the words 'school' and education' in the **title** and **slogan**. These combine to hint that the character is also a teacher.

The **tagline** 'We Don't Need No Education' captures the essence of the story as it implies that the 'School of Rock' will not be a typical school. It is also the chorus line from a famous rock song and tells us that music will form a key part in the film.

There are several other **slogans** which are also effective. 'Accept no Substitutes' makes use of the **imperative** form of the verb, as does 'Take Notes. Coming Soon.' Both slogans use vocabulary typical of a classroom situation. All of the elements above link well to suggest that the film will include a strong musical element in a school or educational **setting**.

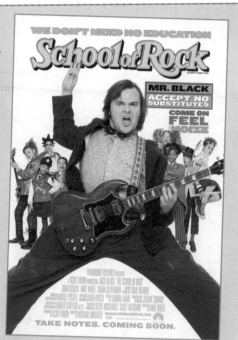

 **L.O. R 4**

Use an appropriate critical vocabulary while responding to literary texts.

Descriptive writing

Key elements of good description include:

- The use of **accurate detail** to create **pictures**.
- **Adjectives** used to describe size, colour, shape and number.
- The use of **figurative language**, e.g. **similes** and **metaphors**.
- **Appeal** to the five **senses**.
- Write a **comprehensive** account of **all key features**.
- Include words that **capture sounds**.

 L.O. R 9

Identify, appreciate and compare the ways in which different literary, digital and visual genres and sub-genres shape texts and shape the reader's experience of them.

Describing visual images

When describing a photograph, it is important to remember a number of important points.

- Always **report the facts** of what you can see.
- Describe the **entire image**: background, middle distance and foreground.
- Mention whether the shot is of an **interior** or **exterior setting**.
- Discuss **light** and **darkness** in the photograph.
- Give details of the **posture** and **expression** of human figures.
- Be as accurate and **precise** as possible.

Sample question and hints

Question 1   20 marks

Describe the image below taken from *The Irish Times* newspaper.

Allow 12 minutes for
20-mark questions.

Hints for approaching questions on an image

- A photograph may be **monochrome (black and white)** or **colour**. It is important to write about this detail. **Portrait** photography is often printed in **black and white** as it helps to emphasise the **emotion** on the human face.

- The **vehicle** in this image is a funeral **hearse** and the dark body of the car acts as a **black frame** for the photo. The shining **chrome rails** on the roof **contrast** with the colour of the car.

- Always include any **written element** of an image. Here the words 'Massey Bros.' appear in the bottom left-hand corner of the side window of the car.

- There is a **long white coffin** with **silver** or **chrome handles** already inside the car. **Several people** can be seen at the rear of the vehicle. The hatch back **door** is **open**. A **woman** holds a **small boy** who is wearing a **white Aran jumper**. The boy is **raising his right hand** to touch his **forehead**. The boy has **blond hair**. He looks like he is **four or five** years of age.

- Sometimes an image might be part of a **newspaper article** and include a **caption** giving further **information** about the photo. The caption for this photo by Mark Condren mentions details of **location** and the tragic **circumstances** but does not identify the deceased person by **name** nor those people who are mourning at the funeral. 'A young relative looks on at the funeral of those who lost their lives in the Carrickmines fire at a traveller halting site.' A well-written caption gives **key facts** but also allows the picture to speak for itself.

Description of setting

Fiction and non-fiction both depend on effective descriptive writing to help to set the scene. You should be prepared to discuss the effects of good description in a passage by focusing on the **impact** of **key words and phrases**.

Suitable vocabulary

Some **key words** apply to both fiction, non-fiction, poetry and drama. Make sure you know what the terms refer to by **learning** the **definitions**.

 L.O. **W 3**

Write for a variety of purposes, for example to:

- analyse
- evaluate
- imagine
- explore, etc.

Alliteration	Repetition of initial consonants in words close to each other.
Antithesis	Two opposite ideas are put together to create a contrast.
Metaphor	Comparing one thing to another thing.
Onomatopoeia	When the sound of a word echoes its meaning.
Sibilance	Repetition of 's' or 'ch' sounds to create a 'hissing' effect.
Simile	A comparison using the words 'like' or 'as'.

Sample questions and answers

Question 1   *10 marks*

Read the passage on the following page and show how two of the following help to create a memorable description:

Allow 6 minutes for 10-mark questions.

- alliteration
- antithesis
- metaphor
- onomatopoeia
- sibilance
- simile

The background

J.A. Baker is a keen birdwatcher who has been following a peregrine falcon as it stalks its prey across the landscape of rural Essex. In the extract on the following page, he observes the motion of both the hunter and his prey.

From *The Peregrine* by J.A. Baker

The tide was rising in the estuary; sleeping waders crowded the saltings; plover were restless. I expected the hawk to drop from the sky, but he came low from inland. He was a skimming black crescent, cutting across the saltings, sending up a cloud of dunlin dense as a swarm of bees. He drove up between them, black shark in shoals of silver fish, threshing and plunging. With a sudden stab down he was clear of the swirl and was chasing a solitary dunlin up into the sky. The dunlin seemed to come slowly back to the hawk. It passed into his dark outline, and did not reappear. There was no brutality, no violence. The hawk's foot reached out, and gripped, and squeezed, and quenched the dunlin's heart as effortlessly as a man's finger extinguishing an insect. Languidly, easily, the hawk glided down to an elm on the island to plume and eat his prey.

Sample answer

1. <u>Simile:</u> The **imagery** of this passage helps us to picture the scene. Baker uses a **simile** to describe the flock of dunlin 'dense as a swarm of bees'. This comparison tells us that he is observing from a distance so that the birds appear black and small like insects. It also suggests that they are flying close together.

2. <u>Metaphor:</u> Baker's **metaphor** of the peregrine as a 'black shark' and the dunlin as 'shoals of silver fish' helps us to **visualise** the **scene**. There is an **important detail** of light and colour but the metaphor also tells us about the relative sizes of the peregrine and the dunlin, and most importantly that one is a strong predator while the other is its helpless quarry.

 **L.O. R 1**

Read texts with fluency, understanding and competence, decoding groups of words/phrases and not just single words.

Question 2   10 marks

Good descriptive writing often appeals to the senses to communicate a scene to us. Read the passage below and identify words and phrases which capture a particular sensation. Write your answers in the spaces provided on the following page.

The background

As a boy of 12 years of age, Robert and his brother are staying at their grandparents' house in the highlands of Scotland.

From *Mountains of the Mind* by Robert MacFarlane

We were staying in the house for the summer. My brother and I were allowed to go anywhere except into the room at the end of the hallway, which was my grandfather's study. We played hide and seek, and I often hid in the big wardrobe in our bedroom. It smelt strongly of camphor, and there was a clutter of shoes on the floor of the wardrobe which made it difficult to stand up in. My grandmother's fur coat hung in it, too, sheathed in thin clear plastic to keep the moths away. It was strange to put a hand out to touch the soft fur and feel the smooth plastic instead.

The best room in the house was the conservatory, which my grandparents called the Sun Room. Its floor was paved with grey flagstones, always cold underfoot, and two of its walls were giant windows.

Even though it was summer, the inside of the house was filled with the cold mineral air of the Highlands, and every surface was always chilly to the touch. When we ate dinner, the chunky silver pieces of cutlery which came out of the dresser were cold in our hands. At night, when we went to bed, the sheets were icy. I would wriggle as far down the bed as I could go, and hold the top sheet down over my head to create an airlock. Then I would breathe as deeply as I could until I had warmed up the bed.

Sight	
Smell	
Sound	
Taste	
Touch	

Analysing a movie sequence

In an earlier section you learned how to **discuss** a **single image**. To recap, it is essential to **observe** all **relevant detail** of **setting** and then dwell on the **subject** that is the **focus** of the image. In a similar way, your powers of observation are called into play when you are asked to **explain** a **scene** or a number of scenes from a film. If you are sitting the Junior Cycle English exam in 2019 or 2020, your **studied film** must come from the following list:

1. *Life Is Beautiful*
2. *Whale Rider*
3. *Bend It Like Beckham*
4. *Son of Rambow*
5. *The Night of the Hunter*
6. *School of Rock*
7. *Spirited Away*
8. *In America*
9. *E.T. the Extra-Terrestrial*
10. *Beasts of the Southern Wild*

In class you have **viewed** and **discussed** a film for your Junior Cycle. In addition to **analysing** characters, plot and key themes you must be clear about how to make sense of a key moment from your film using **the correct terminology** or what is sometimes called the 'Language of Film'.

When selecting a **key moment** to analyse, it is a good idea to take an **early sequence** or series of scenes as these **initial moments** often serve to **establish character** and **setting** in typical ways.

Students taking the exam in 2019 or 2020 have the option to study one of the following instead of a studied film from the prescribed list: A documentary film/a travel text/a biography.

Suitable vocabulary

Acting	Actors' use of posture, movement and dialogue to create character.
Costume	Style, colour and contrasts in clothing hints at personality.
Editing	Cuts between shots or scenes – transitions.
Mise-en-scène	All elements combining to create a fictional world.
Lighting	Colour and intensity created by lighting can establish a mood or atmosphere.
Props	Significant objects carried, held or used by the characters.
Sequence	A series of scenes combining to create a longer episode, e.g. title sequence.
Shots	Views presented on screen – close-up/full shot/long shot/panning.
Sound effects	Noises added to emphasise impact and build action.
Soundtrack	Original songs and music added to underline the mood.

The **title sequence** of any film is all the **action** from the **opening image** up to the **last shot**, showing superimposed **credits, writing** or **titles**. Typically these initial sounds and images combine to:

- Set the scene
- Establish character
- Hook the viewer

Watch the **title sequence** of your chosen film and list your observations under the headings in the table on the following page.

It is important to notice what you **hear** and **see**, but to also **explain** the **impact** it makes in the title sequence. For example, under the first category of **acting**, Jack Black – playing the part of Dewey Finn in the opening sequence of *School of Rock* – **postures** like a rock star, literally **stealing the limelight** from the lead singer on stage.

Technique	Details	Impact
Acting		
Camera angles		
Costumes		
Dialogue		
Props		
Shots		
Sound effects		
Soundtrack		

Sample question and answer

Question 1   25 marks

Show how a sequence from a film you studied helps to create a memorable character on screen.s

Allow 15 minutes for 25-mark questions.

Title: *School of Rock*

Director: *Richard Linklater*

Sample answer

The film I studied is *School of Rock* and the **central character** is Dewey Finn **played** by Jack Black. We are introduced to Dewey in the **title sequence** of the movie. The **hand-held camera** gives the viewer the sensation of walking into a dark nightclub. We feel drawn into this **setting** and become part of the audience at the show. Neon **lighting** typical of this **setting** is used to present the **title** for the film.

The camera **focuses** on Dewey in **close-up**. Jack Blacks' exaggerated **facial expressions** and melodramatic **posturing** begin to upstage the lead singer. He makes use of his guitar and the microphone stand as **key props** in this gradual bid for control.

Watch 'School of Rock Intro Song' on YouTube or DVD.

The **character** commands our attention through his disrobing of his rock-star **costume** and his eventual stage-dive belly-flop. The change in **camera angle** from **low** to **high** suggests a rapid fall from grace and his failure is underlined by the **sound effects** of glass shattering. Dewy Finn rock legend has been brought down to earth with a bang.

EXAMINER'S COMMENT

- Candidate **focuses** on **terms** of the **question** – characterisation on screen.
- Excellent use of **critical vocabulary** to **analyse** title sequence.
- **Precise examples** are used to **illustrate key points** in each paragraph.

MARKS AWARDED: Ex. 25/23 (90–100%) Distinction

If you are sitting the Junior Cycle English exam in 2021–2023, your studied film must come from the following list

1. *Wadjda*
2. *Moonrise Kingdom*
3. *Sing Street*
4. *Whale Rider*
5. *Amadeus* (biopic)
6. *Suffragette*
7. *Hotel Rwanda* (biopic)
8. *The Night of the Hunter*
9. *Kes*
10. *Man on Wire* (documentary, biopic)
11. *Spirited Away*
12. *E.T. the extra-terrestrial*
13. *His and Hers* (documentary)
14. *Hunt for the Wilderpeople*
15. *Beasts of the Southern Wild*

Exam Question 2017 (SEC Junior Cycle Sample 3)

Section A – Appreciating Audience and Register – Faraway Places

For copyright reasons, the publisher is unable to reproduce the extract of NASA astronaut Commander Chris Hadfield's TED talk. This extract is available for download on the State Examination Commission website www.examinations.ie.

Watch 'What I learned from going blind into space' (up to 4:00) on YouTube.

Question 1   20 marks

In your view, what elements of the above talk would have made it engaging for the audience listening? Explain your answer by referring to both the style and the content of the talk.

Question 2   10 marks

The pictures below and on the following page show the settings for three different stories. Choose one of the pictures and write a descriptive paragraph in which you create a picture of the place and give the reader a sense of the mood or atmosphere in that place.

Undiscovered

Exploring Mars

Boundaries

I choose to set my story in the place shown in the picture labelled:

_____

Descriptive paragraph:

_____
_____
_____
_____
_____
_____
_____
_____
_____
_____
_____
_____
_____
_____
_____
_____
_____
_____
_____
_____

3 Understanding the Power of Words: Poetry and Flash Fiction

In this section you will:

- **Learn** how to **discuss poems** and very short **fiction**.
- **Identify** and **explain** key **poetic techniques**.
- **Explore** the importance of the **choice** and **order** of words in a text.
- **Read** sample **questions**, **hints** and sample **answers**.
- Find out what is involved in **comparing** two poems.
- **Respond** to texts, commenting on **language patterns**, **style** and **content**.
- **Compose** your own short piece of **fiction**.

During the course of your Junior Cycle you have **read** many different texts in a variety of **writing styles**. The most memorable writing lives on in the imagination for two reasons: because of **what the writer tells** us, and because of the **words** they use to **express** their **thoughts** and **feelings**.

As an expert **reader**, you are sensitive to both the **meaning** of the words in a written text and also to **how** the **style** of writing produces a **strong impact**.

Appreciating language is about becoming **aware** of the **power** of **words**. It is the skill of recognising how **individual words**, **groups of words** and **patterns of words** affect the **meaning** of a text. Romantic poet Samuel Taylor Coleridge appreciated the importance of choosing the right words when he explained the **difference** between **prose writing** and **poetry**. He said, **prose** is 'words in their best order' while **poetry** is 'the best words in the best order'.

All the texts you will read and discuss in your exam are chosen because a writer has expressed thoughts or feelings in a **unique** way. This section will help you to perfect the **skill of language appreciation**. You will develop your **sensitivity** to **language** by **analysing** the work of others and **creating** original work of your own.

 L.O. R 8

Read texts to understand and appreciate language enrichment by examining an author's choice of words:

- the use and effect of simple figurative language
- vocabulary and language patterns
- images

as appropriate to the text.

Types of questions

In the Junior Cycle exam, appreciation of language can be tested with different types of questions:

1. **Responding** to a **single unseen poem**.
2. **Identifying** specific elements of poetic **technique**.
3. **Evaluating** the overall **impact** of a **poem**.
4. **Comparing** two **poems** in terms of **content** and/or **style**.
5. **Discussing** the effect of **vocabulary choice** in a **story**.
6. Using a **bank** of **words** as **inspiration** for a short piece of **creative writing**.

Areas to revise

Close reading of unseen poetry	Responding to poetry using suitable vocabulary.
Comparing two poems linked by theme	Identifying and comparing their similarities and differences.
Discussing flash fiction	Reading and responding to plot, character and style.
Writing your own original fiction	Creative writing using prompts provided.

Close reading of unseen poetry

For the purposes of the exam, you may need to **read** and **write** about poems you have never seen or thought about before. It is important to remember that your examiner does not expect expert analysis. On the other hand, it is fair and reasonable to test your ability to:

- **Read** a poem **carefully**.
- **Identify** the **topic** or **subject** the poem **explores**.
- **Observe** the **way** the poet uses **words**.
- **Notice** how the words **affect** your own **thoughts** and **feelings**.

key point

Always explain your points, referring to the key words or phrases in the poem.

When writing about poetry, it is vital that you use the **correct language** to **identify** and **explain** the writer's style. You can give **focus** to your revision by reading and learning the **eight key terms** defined in the table on the following page. Remember, it is not enough to simply learn definitions; you must be able to find **examples** and **explain** their **effect** to truly demonstrate skilful reading of poetry.

Suitable vocabulary

Below are key poetic terms to learn and use in your discussion of poetry.

Alliteration	Repetition of consonants close to each other.
Assonance	Repetition of identical vowel sounds in words close to each other.
Colloquial language	Informal language close to the vocabulary of everyday speech.
Contrast	Pointing out and emphasising the differences between people or things.
Dialogue	Words spoken by characters in a poem, story or drama.
Enjambment	When the sense of a line 'runs on' from one line to the next.
Imagery	Images or mental pictures created in a poem.
Metaphor	Comparing one thing to another thing in a poem.

Sample question and answer

Read the following poem by Imtiaz Dharker, in which she celebrates the importance of water to a community, and answer the question on page 43.

Blessing
By Imtiaz Dharker

The skin cracks like a pod.
There never is enough water.

Imagine the drip of it,
the small splash, echo
in a tin mug,
the voice of a kindly god.

Sometimes, the sudden rush
of fortune. The municipal* pipe bursts,
silver crashes to the ground
and the flow has found

a roar of tongues. From the huts,
a congregation: every man woman
child for streets around
butts in, with pots,
brass, copper, aluminium,
plastic buckets,
frantic hands,

and naked children
screaming in the liquid sun,
their highlights polished to perfection,
flashing light,
as the blessing sings
over their small bones.

*Provided by the local council.

Close reading strategy

You must read the poem carefully several times.

1. **Read it** for the **first time** using a **highlighter** to choose five **key words**/phrases.
2. **Underline images**, **similes** or **metaphors** on your second reading.
3. **Pick out** any **sound effects** you recognise the third time you read the poem.

This is a way of **recording** your **thoughts** as you read. In addition, you can **write notes** in the **margin** for yourself expressing your **response** to words and phrases.

The annotated poem below is an example of how to keep track of your initial thoughts and feelings about an unseen poem. **Focus** on what you **notice** or **recognise**. Do not dwell on the lines or words that confuse you.

Unseen poem	Technique	Personal response
Blessing		
By Imtiaz Dharker		
The skin cracks like a pod.	*Contrast*	*imagery highlights impact of water*
There never is enough water.		
Imagine the drip of it,		
the small splash, echo	*Assonance*	*allows us to hear sound of the drops*
in a tin mug,		
the voice of a kindly god.	*Metaphor*	*power and generosity*
Sometimes, the sudden rush		
of fortune. The municipal pipe bursts,		
silver crashes to the ground		
and the flow has found		
a roar of tongues. From the huts,		
a congregation : every man woman	*Alliteration*	*people are rushing, urgent speed*
child for streets around	*Enjambment*	
butts in, with pots,		
brass, copper, aluminium,		
plastic buckets,		
frantic hands,		

and naked children   *Imagery*   *memorable picture of happiness*

screaming in the liquid sun,

their highlights polished to perfection,

flashing light,

as the blessing sings

over their small bones.

 L.O. R 11

Identify and comment on features of English at word and sentence level using appropriate terminology, showing how such features contribute to overall effect.

Question 1

A. Find examples of each the following techniques in the poem 'Blessing':

Alliteration	
Assonance	
Contrast	
Enjambment	
Imagery	
Metaphor	

B. Choose three of the above and write a short paragraph explaining the impact each one makes in the poem.

Sample answer

1. There are several **examples** of **assonance** in the **second stanza**. The same slender 'i' **vowel sound** is **repeated** in the phrase 'drip of it'. Hearing the 'i' sound twice **echoes the effect of droplets landing** on a surface. Also, the phrase 'in a tin' **draws attention** to the **noise** of drops falling into the bottom of a **metal mug**.

2. The poet uses **enjambment** in the lines:

   'every man woman
   child for streets around
   butts in,'

   creating the feeling of a mad scramble for water. By **leaving out punctuation** with the lines ending 'woman' and 'around', Imtiaz Dharker forces the **eye** and the voice to **'run-on' to the next line** as if the reader is rushing like the people in the poem. In this way the **style** of the lines **echoes** the people's urgent movement.

3. In the line 'the voice of a kindly god', the poet is using a **metaphor** to **compare water to a generous divine presence**. The **effect** of this metaphor is

to **emphasise the power** of the water to sustain life. It also encourages us to imagine that the **sound** of a **gentle god** is like the **beautiful noise water makes** as it flows into a cup.

Unseen poetry questions often require you to express your **personal opinion**. Remember to **back up your ideas** with **quotation** from the poem and **explanations**.

More useful vocabulary

The **words** below and their **definition**s are important. Along with the terms you revised earlier, these are the **most common poetic techniques**. When you write about poetry you must **discuss** the poems **using** the **correct words** in a way that **shows** a **clear understanding** of **how** poets **create** certain effects.

Onomatopoeia	When the sound of a word echoes its meaning.
Personification	When an object, idea or animal is described as if it were human.
Rhyme	When two word endings have the same or similar sounds.
Sibilance	The repetition of 's' or 'ch' sounds to create a 'hissing' effect.
Stanza	A separate group of lines in a poem.
Simile	A comparison using the words 'like' or 'as'.
Theme	A key idea explored in a poem.
Tone	A reflection of the writer's attitude or feeling in a poem.

Sample questions and answers

Read the poem 'In Memory of George Best' and answer the questions which follow.

In Memory of George Best

By Dermot Bolger

In one corner of our minds it remains 1969:
Frosted pavements, icy breath, yet our hands thaw

In the thrill of chasing a ball under streetlights,
Voices in the dark calling the names of Best and Law.

A drudge of decades have clogged our arteries,
Yet no matter what occurred, what we have become,

When we see again his feint, his sheer artistry
Thousands of us are instantaneously made young.

key point

Nouns are words that name **people** and **things**. There are four types of nouns: **common nouns**, **proper nouns**, **collective nouns** and **abstract nouns**.

Question 1

a) 'minds/pavements/breath/hands' are examples of which type of **noun**:

Proper	
Common	✓
Abstract	
Collective	

b) 'Best/Law' are examples of which type of **noun**:

Proper	✓
Common	
Abstract	
Collective	

c) 'thrill/artistry' are examples of which type of **noun**:

Proper	
Common	
Abstract	✓
Collective	

Question 2   15 marks

What **images** does the poet recall from his childhood?

Sample answer

The poet remembers **playing football with his friends** in the **streets** in '1969'. The death of George Best reminds him of 'the thrill of **chasing a ball** under streetlights'. As a child he was inspired to play by the 'sheer artistry' of his heroes.

Allow 10 minutes for 15-mark questions.

Another **image** is of the **cold weather** as the children played in spite of the '**frosted** pavements and **icy breath**' of **wintertime**.

Bolger also **creates** for us the **sounds** he heard as he played. He and his pals called out to each other 'the names of **Best and Law**', pretending to be famous soccer players.

EXAMINER'S COMMENT

- **Three relevant points** are made about **'images'** in the poem.
- Each **point** is **developed** in a short **paragraph**.
- The student **illustrates** the **points** well by including **five** relevant **quotations**.

MARKS AWARDED: Ex. 15/15 (90–100%) Distinction

Question 3
15 marks

How would you describe the tone of the poem?

Sample answer

The **tone** or **feeling** of this poem is **nostalgic**. The **death** of his **hero**, George Best, makes the poet **remember the good times** when he was **young**. When he thinks again about 'chasing a ball under streetlights' he feels **happy**.

 L.O. R 3

Use a wide range of reading comprehension strategies appropriate to texts, including digital texts:

- to retrieve information
- to link to previous knowledge
- to follow a process or argument
- to summarise, etc.

The poet also feels **regret** that he is no longer a child **enjoying** the fun of a street game. Since '1969' a 'drudge of decades' has passed and his life is not as **exciting** as it used to be.

I think he feels **surprised** that his hero's 'sheer artistry' can work like magic on so many people who are 'instantaneously made young'. Bolger is **sad** that George Best is dead, but **grateful** that this footballer brought him so much **pleasure** in his life.

EXAMINER'S COMMENT

- The first sentence **identifies** a **tone** of **nostalgia**.
- Feelings of **happiness, regret, excitement, surprise, sadness** and **gratitude** are also identified.
- **Comprehensive description** of the **tone** in the poem.

MARKS AWARDED: Ex. 15/14 (90–100%) Distinction

 exam TIPS

- Always put **titles** in **inverted commas** and use **capitals** for **main words**, e.g. 'In Memory of George Best' by Dermot Bolger
- **Learn** the full **title** and poet's **name**.
- Write in **paragraphs**.
- Answer the **full question**.
- Give your own **personal response**, e.g. 'I like ...
- **Explain** your points (**give reasons**), e.g. '... because'
- Use **correct** poetic **terms** to **analyse**.

Comparing two poems linked by theme

Your **awareness** of **language** also comes into play when **comparing** different poems dealing with a **similar topic** or **theme**. Your teacher will have prepared you by exploring how two poets treat the **same subject matter** in their own **unique** way.

The poems below are popular, probably because we can all relate to certain **experiences from early childhood**.

 L.O. R 2

Read for a variety of purposes:
- learning
- pleasure
- research
- comparison

Sample questions and answers

Question 1   *30 marks (15+15)*

a) Discuss two ways in which the poems are like each other in their treatment of the key idea.

Allow 10 minutes for 15-mark questions.

Read both poems carefully and answer the questions which follow.

A Child Half Asleep	Driving Home at Dusk with Dónal, 4
By Tony Connor	By Don Byrne

A Child Half Asleep
By Tony Connor

Stealthily parting the small-hours silence,
a hardly-embodied figment of his brain
comes down to sit with me
as I work late.
Flat-footed, as though his legs and feet
were still asleep.

He sits on a stool,
staring into the fire,
his dummy dangling.

Fire ignites the small coals of his eyes.
It stares back through the holes
into his head, into the darkness.

I ask him what woke him?
'A wolf dreamed me' he says.

Driving Home at Dusk with Dónal, 4
By Don Byrne

As if you were born again,
your question, about headlights,
and my reply about other cars
needing to see, brought us
together, your smile
in the mirror, that 'Ah, yeah'
bonding us just as much
as the night they handed you over
into my cradled arms.

Your surefooted arrival,
just two days after
your grandfather's funeral,
tears of two kinds
rising in me, and you
taking it in silently,
steadily, as if
to secure me.

Always read a poem carefully and pay attention to the **thoughts and feelings** it **evokes** for you.

Much of our lives now
twin orbits,
catching the odd glimpse
in the rear mirror,
the snug feel of you
into my armpit at night
at storytime.

Always that sure sense
that you and he passed
each other in soul flight,
touched hands for just
long enough for him to say,
'Look after your father,
he's all yours now.'

Sample answer

'A Child Half Asleep' by Tony Connor and 'Driving Home at Dusk with Dónal, 4' by Don Byrne both explore the **theme** of **relationships between parents and their young children**.

Both poets celebrate a tender moment when they are **alone with their child**. Tony Connor is 'working late' when his child 'comes down to sit' with him, while Don Byrne and his son Dónal are 'driving home' alone together. The private family **settings in both** poems help to emphasise the closeness of the connection between these two fathers and their young children.

The two poets also include **dialogue** reporting the words used by each child in the conversation. Tony Connor's final line is his son's magnificent **poetic** declaration 'A wolf dreamed me.' On the other hand, Don Byrne's son Dónal simply replies in a **colloquial** way 'Oh yeah' to his father's explanation of the dipped headlights. In each case the **conversation** reveals the trust and intimacy between parent and child.

15 marks

b) Explain one way in which the poems are different in what they say on that topic. Support the points you make with suitable quotation from the poems.

Sample answer

They **differ** in the way they deal with the **topic** of **parents and their relationship with young children**. In one poem, the parent **cherishes** the **memory** of a surprising and **enlightening conversation**, while in the second poem the parent is reminded of a moment from their **shared past**. In the first poem the father is taken aback by the **unusual expression** 'A wolf dreamed me', emerging as it does from the mind of his drowsy son. On the other hand, the father in the second poem reflects on a less original conversation but imagines his son taking care of him as his dying father once did.

In the second poem, the idea of **parents and their children** is developed in a new way because Dónal's father is also thinking about his own dad. We find out that Dónal was born 'just two days after [his] grandfather's funeral'. The web of care between fathers and sons is **more complex** in the second poem. The **loss of a parent** mixed with the **joy of a new child complicates** the **theme** in the second poem. I think it adds a richness to the theme of parents and their relationships to their children.

Discussing flash fiction

Your **appreciation** of the impact of **language** can be tested by asking you to **read** in any **genre**. Poetry is the 'best words in the best order' and the most memorable poems offer us an **intense experience** of **language**. For that reason it is important to develop the **skills** of **close reading** and **analysis** when dealing with the **condensed style** of **poetry**. **Very short stories** or '**flash fiction**' are like poetry because the genre requires writers to tell their tale in a **small number** of **words**. In this very **limited space**, complex **character, setting** and **plot** are presented without lavish detail. Ancient writers made up very short stories where the characters were animals. **Aesop's fables** always teach a **lesson** about **human foolishness**, but in a **simple storyline** involving **non-human characters**. The **parables** of the New Testament are also very **compressed narratives** with a **clear moral** for the readers to learn.

What unites **poetry, fable, parable** and **flash fiction** is a way of **using very few words** to **communicate** an **intense message** to the reader. The examples below are famous modern **flash fiction** stories. In the remaining pages of this section you will learn how to answer **comprehension questions** on flash fiction and how to **create** your own **very short story**.

Rumour has it that Ernest Hemingway, the famous American novelist, was challenged to write the **briefest short story possible**. He took very little time to come up with the following tiny tragedy:

 'For sale: baby shoes, never worn.'

Whether this is Hemingway's original story or not, it displays all the **typical traits** of **flash fiction**:

- The entire **narrative** is told using **very few words**.
- A single sentence expresses the **full story**.
- **Character, setting** and **plot** are **hinted at** but **not developed.**
- **Mood** is **evoked** in an **intense** but **brief moment.**
- The **reader** is given very **little detail.**
- We are **forced** to **imagine** what might be left out.

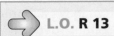 **L.O. R 13**

Appreciate a variety of registers and understand their use in the written context.

Sample question and hints

Read the following story by Lydia Davis and answer the questions which follow.

The Outing
By Lydia Davis

> An outburst of anger near the road, a refusal to speak on the path, a silence in the pine woods, a silence across the old railroad bridge, an attempt to be friendly in the water, a refusal to end the argument on the flat stones, a cry of anger on the steep bank of dirt, a weeping among the bushes.

Question 1

a) 'anger' is an example of which type of noun:

Proper	
Common	
Abstract	✓
Collective	

b) **How** does the writer **create** an **interesting setting** for her story 'The Outing'? Would you agree that **character** is **suggested** but not fully **developed**? **Explain** your answer.

c) 'Good flash fiction depends on a **strong clear plot**.' **To what extent** does 'The Outing' **illustrate** this point?

Hints

- 'An outburst of anger' and a 'cry of anger' appear in the story. While the **common nouns** 'outburst' and 'cry' refer to **concrete** sounds which can be heard, 'anger' is an **emotion** and a different type of noun. It is **not** something **tangible**. Choose the word that best describes this type of noun that is hard to put your finger on!

- Even though flash fiction does not normally allow the writer much room for detail, in this story Lydia mentions **eight different features** of a **rural setting**. This suggests a **journey** through a **mysterious landscape**, the **destination** for an 'outing' or day trip. Discuss this **technique** of **teasing** the reader by giving **just enough information** to allow us to picture the scene but also **forcing** us to **imagine** a great deal.

- We can tell there are at least **two characters** as the story involves a **confrontation**, a **stand-off**, **sulking** and a failed **reconciliation**. We also pick up on the **intense emotion** being **expressed** by the characters. What makes it so mysterious is we never find out **why** this is happening or what the **final outcome** will be.

- There are **eight key moments** in this narrative. Each one follows in a **logical sequence**. The **emotional response** of the characters gives it a strong **intensity**. You could argue that the story is **mysterious** when it comes to **who they are** and **why they are in conflict** and for that reason it is not crystal clear.

Writing your own original fiction

A heightened **awareness of language** will also help you to be **original** and **fresh** in your **creative writing**. The short time available to you for the Junior Cycle English exam means that you will **not** have **sufficient time** to compose a **fully developed short story**. In the course of your Junior Cycle, you have studied several excellent examples of short stories where **realistic characters** confront serious problems and find themselves in **situations** of **complex conflict**. This can be highly **entertaining** to read and a real challenge for the writer. Because this type of writing task requires a lot of time, it is something best left to class work or your written assignment **collection of work**.

In the exam, however, it is possible that you will be asked to write a **key paragraph** from a **short story**, or even challenged to compose a **very short piece of fiction** like a **parable**, **fable** or a piece of **flash fiction**. In the event that you face this type of task, the following guidelines will apply:

- Use the **space** provided to **plan** and **draft**.
- **Begin** the story in the **middle** of a dramatic event.
- Keep the **action simple**.
- **Don't** have **too many characters**.
- **Avoid lavish detail**, e.g. too many adjectives.
- **Hint** at **character** and **emotion**.
- **Write long** and **pare** the story back.

Punctuate! Every sentence must begin with a **capital letter** and end with **a full stop, exclamation** mark or **question** mark.

Sample question and answer

Question 1

Use the words in the diagram on the following page to write a short piece of fiction. You may use all the vocabulary from the word cloud and any additional words necessary to complete your paragraph.

Write a single paragraph:

a) An opening paragraph for a short story

OR

b) A very short piece of flash fiction

Use the optional rough work space provided to plan and draft your work.

A paragraph is a group of sentences with a united purpose.

ask arms hand odd
made bunch secure voice best
sure breath chasing names time rear
rush bones whish bursts silver minds
say reply endless streets crashes stairs naked
one father smile municipal glimpse night
echo together around brass
sense thousands surefooted needing gives two
orbits tin grandfather's aluminium liquid soul
top headlights sometimes ball see
child consolation congregation remains
like light catching sheer snug
skin perfection yet funeral voices
twin arrival funeral screaming law
lives steadily icy storytime never
clogged children highlights buckets fits
kinds artistry flashing days
long armpit feint polished pots
found question feel small cradled pipe
cracks plastic instantaneously occurred sings
palm taking pavements streetlight brought yeah
enough frosted carpetway arteries matter thrill mug
just copper bonding blessing steep
man corner touched decades tongues tears
thaw kindly imagine handed sun
water ground become young
god flow dark woman every look
pod now roar born

hands **silently** **mirror**
much **take** **small**
Calling **drudge** **cars**

exam focus

If a word bank or word cloud is provided for your creative writing, think of it as a treasure trove of helpful suggestions. Use the words and add some of your own.

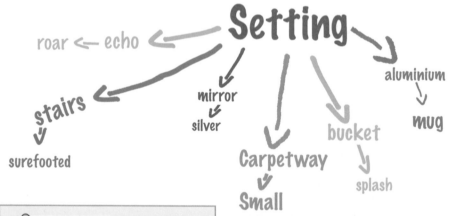

roar ← echo ← **Setting**
stairs mirror aluminium
surefooted silver mug
bucket
Carpetway splash
Small

L.O. **W 1**

Demonstrate understanding that there is a clear purpose for all writing activities and be able to

- plan
- draft
- re-draft
- edit

as appropriate.

When you have **outlined** a **few ideas** in the **rough work**, try to **write a sentence** using some of the **vocabulary provided** and **extra detail** from your own **imagination**. Remember, for a short task like this you can **draft** and **edit** your work.

For the opening paragraph of a story, there are five key features:
1. **Hook** the reader – engage their curiosity in a mysterious or dramatic situation.
2. **Set** the **scene** – paint a picture of where the action is taking place.
3. **Create** a strong **mood** – use detail to build a clear feeling at the start of the story.
4. Introduce **character** – who is the main person in this narrative?
5. **Narrative** voice: First or third person? Choose a perspective and stick to it.

Sample answer: An opening paragraph for a short story

The dark carpetway was silent. She could dimly see the stairs ahead. She climbed surefooted, at the same time calling out grandfather's name. All she heard was the echo of drops. Was it water falling into an aluminium bucket? No, a softer sound. In the bathroom, in front of a cracked mirror, raindrops splashed in the tiny silver mug.

EXAMINER'S COMMENT

- The student writer here has used the **vocabulary** from the word cloud to **set the scene**. The 'carpetway', 'stairs' and 'bathroom' are all features of a house, the **setting** for this short story.
- We are also **introduced** to the central female **character** and an important **relationship** as she calls out to her grandfather.
- The **mood** is **tense** as the main character makes her way through the empty house. The reader is **mystified** and maybe even **anxious** for the character's safety.
- There is a **contrast** between the **silence** of the hallway and the **echo** of the raindrops in the silver mug.
- The narrative **point of view** is third person, but the reader is limited to the main character's vision of what is taking place.

Sample answer: A very short piece of flash fiction

The second sample paragraph is modelled on the style of Lydia Davis' flash fiction story 'The Outing'. Notice how the student tells an entire story using only five sentences.

Small Funeral

Streetlights on the corner highlight cracks in the pavement. Children rush from flashing headlights. A woman screams in the frosty night. Her frantic tears questioning the perfection of an icy god. A frantic congregation cradles the child, wishing for consolation.

Exam Question 2017 (SEC Junior Cycle Sample 3)

Section D – Appreciating Language – Poetry – Inspired by Place

Read the following poem by Seamus Heaney and answer the questions that follow:

Lovers on Aran
By Seamus Heaney

The timeless waves, bright, sifting, broken glass,
Came dazzling around, into the rocks,
Came glinting, sifting from the Americas

To possess Aran.
Or did Aran rush
to throw wide arms of rock around a tide
That yielded with an ebb, with a soft crash?

Did sea define the land or land the sea?
Each drew new meaning from the waves' collision.

Sea broke on land to full identity.

Question 1 — 20 marks

Identify a line or phrase in the poem where the poet uses each of the following poetic techniques and explain why you think the poet uses the technique:

Contrast

_____

_____

_____

_____

_____

Personification

_____

_____

_____

_____

Tone

_____

_____

_____

_____

Assonance

_____

_____

_____

Enjambment

_____

_____

_____

Question 2
10 marks

What do you think is the message in this poem? Explain your answer.

_____

_____

_____

_____

_____

_____

_____

_____

_____

_____

_____

_____

_____

_____

_____

Question 3
10 marks

Evaluate how one of the techniques named in Question 1 of this section helps to convey the message you have identified in the poem.

_____

_____

_____

_____

_____

_____

_____

_____

_____

_____

_____

_____

_____

_____

_____

Question 4   *30 marks*

Choose any two poems you have studied that you feel give you a strong sense of the places in which they are set.

Give the poets' names and the titles of their poems.

Marks are awarded for giving full titles and names with correct spelling.

Title poem 1:	Title poem 2:
Poet's name:	Poet's name:

In your view, which one of the poets was more successful in conveying a sense of place in his/her poem? Support your analysis with detailed reference to both of your nominated poems.

_____

_____

_____

_____

_____

_____

_____

_____

_____

_____

_____

_____

_____

_____

Question 5   *10 marks*

(a) Imagine you are writing a poem. Outline the message you would like to convey in your poem.

    The poem could be about something personal, social, universal or a combination of all three.

_____

_____

_____

_____

_____

_____

_____

_____

_____

_____

_____

_____

(b) Suggest an image you would use in your poem as outlined above, and explain
     why you feel that it would be an appropriate image to use.

_____

_____

_____

_____

_____

_____

_____

_____

_____

_____

_____

_____

4 Ways of Reading: Infographics, Advertising and Fiction

aims

In this section you will:
- **Learn** about a **variety** of **reading strategies.**
- Practise **reading** to **find information.**
- Revise **following** the **logic** of an **argument.**
- **Evaluate** the **methods** of **presentation** in **visual texts.**
- **Critically analyse advertisements** using **suitable** language.
- **Practise** the skill of **comprehending non-fiction.**
- Read and **discuss** a key moment from **fiction.**
- Study **sample questions, hints** and **sample answers.**

You are surrounded by the **written word.** On your mobile phone, in schoolbooks, on billboard posters and in a **multitude** of other ways you **encounter language** every day. The words, sentences and paragraphs you see all require the **skill of reading** in order for you to understand what is being communicated to you. Sometimes the **message is simple** and short like a **text message**; sometimes it is **longer** and **more complex** like a **chapter** in a **textbook.** While the basic skill of making sense of individual words is common to all forms of reading, **different types** of **texts** demand **specific ways** of **reading.**

 **L.O. R 12**

Understand how
- word choice
- syntax
- grammar
- text structure

may vary with context and purpose.

Different styles of reading

There are many **different ways** of **making sense** of the **words** and **sentences** we read every day. The table on the following page lists **eight** of the **most common methods** we use. They vary depending on the **length of time** and the **degree of attention** you give to something you are reading. It is important to know the **skill demanded** by each one of these different ways of reading, and to use the **appropriate** strategy for each **reading task** you are given in your exam.

 L.O. R 3

Use a wide range of reading comprehension strategies appropriate to texts, including digital texts:
- to retrieve information
- to link to previous knowledge
- to follow a process or argument
- to summarise, etc.

Skim	Read quickly, especially headings and captions, to get the gist of something.
Scan	Check a passage for essential key words or phrases.
Repeat	Read and read again more carefully.
Close reading	Pay attention to all elements of the vocabulary and structure.
Highlight	Pick out key words and phrases.
Comprehension	Relate it to what you already know.
Summarise	Select key points from a longer passage and express it simply.
Infer	Read between the lines for meaning.

Think about the following different situations when you use the skill of reading. **Rank** the **list** in **order** based on which type of reading requires the greatest amount of **time** and **attention. 1** = the least and **8** = the most.

	Browsing the **magazines** in the **dentist's waiting room.**
	Checking the 'what's on' web page of your **local cinema site.**
	Reading the **full match report** of a big game in the **local paper.**
	Revising the **climax** of your Junior Cycle **novel.**
	Following a set of **instructions** on the **recipe** for a meal.
	Running through the **list** of **snaps** on your **Snapchat.**
	Filling out an **application form** for a part-time job.
	Reading a **letter** or **email** from your Spanish **penpal.**

In this section you will revise the **skill** of **reading** in a **variety** of ways. The exercise on the previous page reminds you that your method of reading will change depending on the **situation** you are in and the **form** of the **written text** you are dealing with. In your exam you will have to make sense of **shorter written texts** like poems, **longer passages** of fiction and non-fiction, and highly **visual texts** like infographics and advertisements. These reading skills are tested in all exams in every subject, so **focused revision** of **reading strategies** for Junior Cycle English will help you across the **full range** of exams at all levels.

Types of questions

In the Junior Cycle exam, reading comprehension strategies can be tested with different types of questions:

- **Making sense** of **infographics.**
- Critical **analysis** of **advertisements.**
- **Comprehending** passages of **non-fiction.**
- **Responding** to fiction and **identifying elements** of genre.

Suitable vocabulary

Key words below are suitable for explaining what is happening in a visual text like an infographic, advertisement or newspaper page. Learn the words and their definitions. Make sure to use them correctly in your answers.

Chart	Information presented in the form of a table or grid.
Copy	The written words or sentences used on a poster.
Data	Facts collected and presented to prove a point.
Font	A specific style of typeface in a certain size.
Graphic	Pictures or images used to illustrate something.
Icon	A simple sign that looks like the thing it represents.
Statistics	Information presented as numbers or percentages.
Symbol	An object that represents something else and provokes emotions.

Making sense of infographics

In its simplest form, **reading** is all about **getting** the **information** you need. **Infographics** are highly **visual texts** that present **facts** in **clear** and **interesting** ways. They are **easy** to understand because:

- Key **data** is shown using **colourful graphs, charts** or **diagrams**.
- All **relevant detail** is supplied on a **single page** or **poster**.
- There is a **flow** of **ideas** from one **element** of the infographic to the next.
- **Graphics** are used to help us to understand the **words**.

Compare the **key words** in the chart above to the **graphic** on the right. Notice how much more **attractive** the information appears when it is presented using **colour** and the **various shapes** of **icons** and **symbols**.

- It is a great deal easier to **skim** the graphic and **pick out** the **main points**.
- Sentences are **short** and **simple**.
- **Headings** in **BOLD black** font **contrast** with the **orange background**.
- **Different colours** are used for each **symbol** or **icon**.
- **Layout** and **space** makes the **message clear**.

There are many **advantages** to the use of infographics. They are an efficient way to communicate **key information quickly. Symbols** and **icons** often have a **universal meaning** which helps **overcome** any **language barrier** for an international audience. Studies have shown that **readers** will **remember** a message that includes **visual** or **graphic** elements **better** than **pure text**.

 **L.O. R 9**

Identify, appreciate and compare the ways in which different literary, digital and visual genres and sub-genres shape texts and shape the reader's experience of them.

WAYS TO READ AN INFOGRAPHIC
POSTER

SYMBOLS

Posters use symbols like this peace logo to represent key ideas. Distinctive graphics communicate more powerfully than words.

CHARTS

Statistics depicted through simple charts help readers to process a great deal of data in one easily read image.

REMEMBER

FONTS are Fun!

STYLE OF PRINT AND SIZE CATCH THE EYE

PRINTED TEXT STYLE

There are thousands of fonts to choose from. The style and size of the letters can keep the reader engaged by using a variety of types. Some fonts are serious, others are casual and suggest fun.

ICONS

Long-established icons have the advantage that they can speak to many different nationalities because the message works by means of a clear and logical graphic.

MAPS

Information about the global impact of a problem can be visualised by means of a coloured map. Hot spots or problem areas are colour coded.

COPY

TEXT
**TEXT TEXT TEXT
TEXT TEXT
TEXT TEXT TEXT**

text text text

TEXT

All graphics and images need to be anchored by some text or written language. The words help to fix or anchor the meaning of the visual elements in the message.

exam Q

Sample questions and answers

TRENDS

- It seems to be a common feature of YA dystopias for the protagonist to be female. Although this may be down to the fact...

- It also seems common for the authors to be female too. Maybe the authors feel more comfortable writing a character of the same gender (although not the case for Scott Westerfield) or perhaps this is down to the likability of a strong female lead.

- The dystopian societies in which the books are set are often split into 'districts' or 'factions' (like with The Hunger Games, Divergent and to a lesser degree Legend).

- Most of the series have a recognisable symbol (whether it be part of the cover or mentioned often throughout the book). For instance, when you thing "Hunger Games" you think "Mockingjay".

- Love triangles are still extremely common, and most YA dystopias feature either one of them or just a single love interest.

- A lot of (if not all) YA dystopians are trilogies. Even the Uglies series, which comprises of four novels, is referred to as a trilogy + companion novel.

Are we sick of these common trends yet, or are they only common because they work? :)

Feed Me Books Now Infographic (http://feedmebooksnow.blogspot.co.uk)

Question 1   5 marks

Study the above infographic on young adult dystopian fiction carefully, then complete the following sentences using only the information provided.

(3)

Allow 3 minutes for 5-mark questions.

a) Who is the central character in *Divergent*?   *Tris*

b) How many young adult series are presented in the infographic?   *Six*

c) Which story is set against a background of international conflict?   *Legend*

d) Only one of the series is written by a man. Which one?   *Uglies*

e) All of the named stories have love as a central theme.
   Write either T for true or F for false in the box provided.   [T]

f) Most young adult dystopian fictions are serial stories.
   Write either T for true or F for false in the box provided.   [T]

Question 2

5 marks

Study this infographic on the problem of water damage to digital devices carefully, then complete the following sentences using only the information provided.

A. The longest recorded rain storm took place in:

   Hawaii

B. The capital city with the highest average rainfall is:

   Berlin

C. A device's IP rating gives information about protection from damage

   from: *water*

   and: *dust*

D. The Xperia Z2 and Z2 tablet are made by:

   Sony

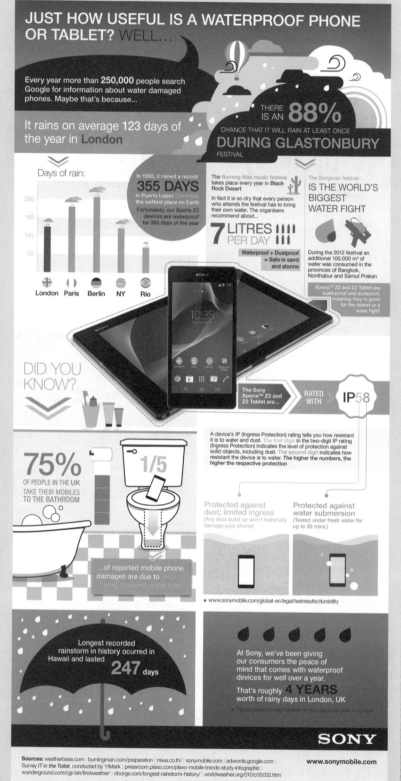

Question 3
20 marks

Infographics are a popular and successful way of communicating facts and data. Do you agree that using an infographic to sell smartphones and tablets is a clever marketing idea? Explain your answer.

Allow 12 minutes for 20-mark questions.

Sample answer

I agree that this advertisement by Sony for their smartphones and tablets uses infographics in a clever way. The first thing I noticed was the **heading** *'Just How Useful Is A Waterproof Phone or Tablet?'* When we read this it looks like the poster is going to provide **facts** and **figures** about water damage and electronic devices. Much of the detail does just that, for example the **panel** telling us that '75% of people in the UK take their mobiles to the bathroom'. This **statistic** is just one of several relevant pieces of **information**. We feel we can **trust** the **data** because the small print at the end of the infographic names the **independent source** for the **figures**.

L.O. W 12

Demonstrate an understanding of how

- syntax
- grammar
- text structure
- and word choice

may vary with context and purpose.

The clever **trick** is to **embed** an **ad** for Sony in a document that looks like it is made up of **pure information**. We are given **facts** about the Xperia in the form of the **IP ratings**. Nowhere in the ad does it claim that the Sony devices are the most waterproof or offer the best protection from damage by dust, but the **implication** is clear that Sony are the best. The **company logo** is discreetly placed at the end in the right corner, but **graphics** of the products **dominate** the centre of the ad.

This **advertisement** is clever because a **biased opinion** about one company's product is communicated in a document which presents **neutral facts** that can be **proven**. Its design and style belong to a genre that readers associate with trustworthy information.

More suitable vocabulary

The terms and definitions on the following page are useful for discussing media, especially advertisements. Learn them and make sure to use them correctly for analysis of visual texts.

L.O. R 11

Identify and comment on features of English at word and sentence level using appropriate terminology, showing how such features contribute to overall effect.

Caption	A title or explanation for a picture or illustration.
Design	Layout and organisation of elements.
Emotive language	Words chosen to bring out strong feelings.
Endorsement	Celebrity used to make it popular.
Logo	Symbols standing for a brand or organisation.
Slogan	Catchy, short phrase – easy to remember.
Target audience	Aiming at a specific group of people.
Use of colour	Colour scheme establishes mood.

Critical analysis of advertisements

When we read **infographics** we **scan** the poster for **key facts** and **figures**. This **way of reading** is different from the style of reading we use for making sense of advertisements. Because both genres use **visual** or **graphic elements**, we are influenced by the **imagery**. The **purpose** of **advertisements** is different from infographics, however. Ads aim to **change our behaviour** by **persuading** us, often trying to get us to buy a product or service. The key factor is our **response**. We read **infographics** looking for **factual data**; we respond to **ads** with our **emotions**.

Advertising is about using a variety of methods to **manipulate** the **feelings** of the reader. When we read an ad in a magazine, we can be **tricked** into believing certain claims about a product if we are not careful.

 L.O. R 8

Read texts to understand and appreciate language enrichment by examining

- an author's choice of words
- the use and effect of simple figurative language
- vocabulary and language patterns
- images

as appropriate to the text.

 **exam focus**

Explain your points clearly. **Give reasons** and **evidence** to **support** the **opinions** you express.

 exam Q

Sample question and hints

Question 1

Look at the advertisement on the following page and answer the questions which follow.

A. Comment on the impact this advert makes on you, referring to each of the following:

- Graphic
- Copy
- Slogan
- Emotive language

The **target audience** is the specific group of people an advertisement is addressing.

Would you give £5 to save Harrison from a slow, painful death?

Harrison suffers from a disease called Duchenne Muscular Dystrophy. It will gradually disable him and eventually kill him. There is no cure, no treatment and very little hope. Harrison's Fund is dedicated to raising money to fund research into a cure or treatment so that we can buy him and others like him some time. This isn't Harrison by the way, this is a picture of a dog I found on the internet. Harrison is my eight year old son. I used this image because people in Britain are more likely to donate to save an animal than a child with Duchenne. Sorry if you feel tricked, my son is dying and I'll do whatever it takes to save him.

Please help us by texting 'Make24 £5' to 70070 harrison's fund

#MakeTime fighting duchenne muscular dystrophy

Hint: A.

The **graphic** is part of the **trick** here. Look at the **camera angle**, the dog's **posture** and **expression**. What **feelings** does the picture try to **evoke**? How does the **placement** of the photo in the top corner **influence** the way you read the **copy** at the end? Why is there a great deal of **blank space** surrounding the **graphic**? Write about the **effect** these details have on your **emotions**.

B. The copy or text in this advert is written in the first person. What is the effect of this on the reader?

> **Hint: B.**
>
> The **first four sentences** present the **facts** about Harrison and his condition in a **neutral** way. Once the word **'I'** is used the communication between the ad and the reader becomes more **personal** and **intimate**. Think about why Harrison's father focuses on himself and his dying son.

C. Write a short speech for or against the following motion:

'Charities are right to use shock tactics to raise awareness of serious issues.'

> **Hint: C.**
>
> In your short speech think about whether you **agree** or **disagree** with shock tactics in advertising. Once you have chosen to argue in favour or against, **stick to your position**. Use detail from this advertising campaign to **support** your **point**s. **Give examples** from other ads if you can think of suitable campaigns. Remember to **be confident** and **defend your opinion**. Good debate speeches emphasise points by using **rhetorical questions, emotive language** and **repetition**. If you can think of a **catchy slogan** to finish your speech, use it to end in a forceful and memorable way.

exam focus

Never attempt **extra questions** in your exam. You will run out of time.

Comprehending passages of non-fiction

The skill in answering comprehension questions is to **focus on what you know** or can **guess** and to block out those phrases you struggle to understand fully. This type of reading relies on having a good **sense** of the **meaning** based on the **context** of the writing.

Prose non-fiction usually combines **factual** elements with phrases that express the **opinion** of the writer. It is important to pay attention and notice the **difference** between objective data and one individual's **personal judgement**.

When a writer sets out to **prove a point**, the quality of the **argument** depends on:

- Providing **good-quality evidence** to back up claims made.
- Making **reasonable connections** between points.
- Arriving at **logical conclusions** based on a **solid development** of ideas.

Close critical analysis of writing means that the **level** of **attention** you pay rewards you with **insight** into the text. **Reading** in this way helps you to **focus** both on **what** the **writer** is **saying** and **how** he/she **expresses** those **ideas**.

key point

Be **critical**. Learn to **separate fact** from **opinion**.

Sample question and hints

Question 1

Read the film review below and answer the questions which follow.

La La Land review: You'll fall in love with the movies again.

By Rohan Naahar

They say the world is dying. They say movies are dead. And they say movie musicals are definitely dead. But there is a cure to this savagery; there is an antidote to this absurdity. It is a movie. It is a musical. It is a musical about movies. It's called *La La Land* and it is here to save your life.

But it won't come to you. You must go to it. You have been wronged far too often, I know; the movies have wronged us all. They have stood us up, left us alone on rainy curbs, but you must put your faith in them, one last time, if only to restore it. You must run to *La La Land*.

It is the story of two dreamers, lost in the City of Stars. He is an aspiring jazz pianist, and she, a hopeful actor with posters of Ingrid Bergman on her wall. Their paths cross, again and again and again in a montage of expertly choreographed numbers as they navigate the magic realism of *La La Land*, and struggle with their hopes and dreams in a city that can be as **stifling** as it is inspiring.

Save for a major upset, *La La Land* will win the Academy Award for Best Picture in February 2017 – not because it should – but because it absolutely must.

From its **euphoric** opening number, set on a Los Angeles freeway, to its final, **melancholic** moments, inside a jazz club; there is not a single moment, not a single glint in the eye, a single smile, a single swish of the dress that doesn't completely envelope you with its **irrepressible** charm. It'll sweep you off your feet, and for two hours, it'll make you fall in love with the movies again.

It might even have the power to single-handedly revive the dying theatre-going experience. It may not be able to save the musical, but for as long as it exists – as long as movies exist – it will ensure that the respect this genre deserves is given to it, even as it takes its last bow, and limps off the stage, having danced to the bitter end.

And for as long as every Friday brings with it new attractions at the local theatre, Ryan Gosling and Emma Stone will be remembered as one of the most **iconic** romantic couples in Hollywood history, just like Humphrey Bogart and Lauren Bacall, or, keeping with the musical theme, Fred Astaire and Ginger Rogers.

There's something enchanting about watching Ryan Gosling's face, isn't there ... bathed in the neon of a Los Angeles night, and dripping in the magic hour twilight of its days. With more classics on his CV than most actors can manage in five-decade-long careers, can there be any doubt now that Ryan Gosling is a movie star in the league of Brando, De Niro, Jimmy Stewart and Cary Grant? I pity the person who walks away from this film, and its two central performances, not having been utterly astounded by its brilliance.

But who do we kneel before?

Shot by Linus Sandgren in Cinemascope (!), and on film (!), so beautifully that you could blindly pick any frame of *La La Land*, and frame it on your wall – it's almost as if the camera is dancing with them. Los Angeles has never looked so good, and neither have its many iconic, cinematic locations that the movie twists and twirls between. Griffith Observatory, Angel's Flight, Chateau Marmont ... They're all **venerable** old movie characters now. It was good to see them again.

But director Damien Chazelle, that champion of cinema ... In times like these, when most people prefer staying at home, has given us a reason to march to the theatres once again. You could always watch *La La Land* on your mobile phone or laptop, but to experience it on the biggest screen possible is an opportunity not to be missed. And on IMAX, it was overwhelming. There was applause, there were groans, there was laughter. And there were tears.

Chazelle is leading the fight to preserve the magic of the movies. His previous film *Whiplash* was my favourite of 2014. *La La Land* is one of my favourites of all time. Depending on how life has treated you, its final moments will be either devastating or irrecoverably shattering. It's one of the finest sequences ever put on film.

exam focus

Read the passage carefully as the context may help to reveal the meaning.

But now, it is time to wait, it is time to consume mediocrity that will surely kill us one day. But this time we wait with renewed faith. Perhaps it'll be another year till something as great as this comes around. Perhaps it'll be two. Perhaps we'll be waiting all our lives. But at least now, we know that it is coming. There is hope yet. The movies are alive. You are alive.

1) **Adjectives** are words that tell us something about a noun. There are six adjectives printed in **bold** the passage above. Write a short explanation of each word in the space provided.

   a) stifling _____

   b) euphoric _____

   c) melancholic _____

d) irrepressible _____

e) iconic _____

f) venerable _____

2) In each case write the letter corresponding to the correct answer in the box.
   The film **genre** of *La La Land* is:
   A. Western
   B. Thriller
   C. Musical

   Which one of the following landmarks is **not** mentioned in the review?
   A. Griffith Observatory
   B. Universal Studios
   C. Chateau Marmont

   La La Land was **directed** by:
   A. Damien Chazelle
   B. Robert De Niro
   C. Linus Sandgren

   The reviewer **highly recommends** watching the film:
   A. On a laptop
   B. On your smartphone
   C. In the cinema

3) The reviewer Rohan Naahar makes an unusual claim in the opening paragraph when he writes that *La La Land* is 'here to save your life'. Evaluate the evidence he offers in the review to prove that this is an exceptional movie. Quote specific claims or observations and write your own evaluation in the space provided.

key point

Beware of **bias** in the media! **Bias** is when only **one side** of the story is being told.

Hint

Find statements made about *La La Land* and check to see if facts are supplied to back up those points. Beware of **exaggeration** or **hyperbole** on the part of this reviewer!

Point 1._____

Evaluation: _____

_____

_____

Point 2. _____

Evaluation:_____

_____

_____

Point 3. _____

Evaluation:_____

_____

_____

Close reading of fiction

In the course of your first three years at second level school you have **read** at least **three novels** and several **short stories**. The main purpose of this type of **reading** is for **pleasure**. We **enjoy** stories because they invite us to **escape** to weird and wonderful **places** with memorable **characters** where exciting **adventures** take place.

Before you do your Junior Cycle it is important to ask yourself the following questions about the **stories you have read**:

L.O. R 7

Select key moments from texts and give thoughtful value judgements on:

- the main character
- a key scene
- a favourite image from a film, a poem, etc.

- What was your **favourite novel** or **short story**?
- **Who** wrote it?
- Who was the **main character**?
- What **problem** did the **hero face** in the story?
- **How** did the hero **cope** with a **difficult situation**?
- **Why** did you find the story **enjoyable** or **entertaining**?
- Was it because of:
  - the **plot**?
  - the **setting**?
  - the **characters**?
  - the **themes explored**?
  - the **mood** or **atmosphere** created?
  - the **genre**?

You will need to have **quality information** available to write about some aspect of your **favourite story**. It is vital to have **clear opinions** that you can **support** with **high-quality evidence** from the **text**.

When **revising** your **novel** or **short story** focus on the following:
  a) The **opening moment** of the story.
  b) A **climax** or moment of high tension.
  c) How the **story ends**.

Revising fiction means **re-reading key moments**, paying attention to both **action** or **plot** and the way the storyteller is using **language**.

- **Make notes** in the **margins** of the text and in your **notes copy**.
- Write down **observations** about the **characters**, their **actions** and **motives**.
- Select **key lines** of **dialogue**.
- Keep a **track** of **changes** in the **mood** of the passage.
- Highlight **individual words** or phrases that have a **specific impact**.
- Identify the type of **vocabulary** used by the writer and its **effect on you**.
- **Pay attention** to your **thoughts** and **feelings** as they develop while you are reading.

Sample question, hints and annotated climax

Question 1

From the novels you studied for your course, identify one which has a memorable and successful climax.

Give the title and author.

a. Title: To Kill a Mockingbird

b. Author: Harper Lee

c. Write a brief summary of the action in the climactic moment.

> **Hint**
>
> Write a paragraph of 100–150 words **outlining** the **sequence** of **events** in the passage.

d. Explain what makes the climax a successful moment of mounting tension.

> **Hint**
>
> Use the notes below and on the following pages to discuss **three ways** in which **tension** is **created** and **increased**.

Scout's own childish narrative is told in **colloquial** language, e.g. 'tusslin' 'bammin' and 'hollered'. This makes the story **realistic** and **communicates** the young girl's **emotion**.

'Then all of a sudden somethin' grabbed me an' mashed my costume ... think I ducked on the ground ... heard a tusslin' under the tree sort of ... they were bammin' against the trunk, sounded like. Jem found me and started pullin' me toward the road. Some – Mr. Ewell yanked him down, I reckon. They tussled some more and then there was this funny noise – Jem hollered ...' I stopped. That was Jem's arm.

'Anyway, Jem hollered and I didn't hear him any more an' the next thing – Mr. Ewell was tryin' to squeeze me to death, I reckon … then somebody yanked Mr. Ewell down. Jem must have got up, I guess. That's all I know … '

> The word 'somebody' is deliberately **vague**. It **creates** an air of **mystery** and makes us wonder about the identity of the helpful stranger.

> Scout is the storyteller or witness and Heck Tate and Atticus the audience. Heck's impatience to find out what happens next adds to the **suspense** of the climax by **increasing tension**.

'And then?' Mr. Tate was looking at me sharply.

'Somebody was staggerin' around and pantin' and – coughing fit to die. I thought it was Jem at first, but it didn't sound like him, so I went lookin'

Suspense is when the **audience** is made to feel **uncertain** or **curious** about what will **happen next**.

> Scout's testimony is filled with **verbs**. This multitude of **high-energy action words** makes the story **exciting** for the reader. We are being told that a **great deal of action** took place over a **short period of time**.

for Jem on the ground. I thought Atticus had come to help us and had got wore out – '

'Who was it?'

'Why there he is, Mr. Tate, he can tell you his name.'

> The **dialogue** is almost **interview style** and Scout's answer comes as a shock to the reader – the mystery rescuer is present in the room.

As I said it, I half pointed to the man in the corner, but brought my arm down quickly lest Atticus reprimand me for pointing. It was impolite to point.

He was still leaning against the wall. He had been leaning against the wall when I came into the room, his arms folded across his chest. As I pointed he brought his arms down and pressed the palms of his hands against the wall. They were white hands, sickly white hands that had never seen the sun, so white they stood out garishly against the dull cream wall in the dim light of Jem's room.

> A highly **detailed** description. Character's **posture** and the condition of his pale hands are emphasised. **Setting** is semi-dark, making it hard to see him.

I looked from his hands to his sand-stained khaki pants; my eyes travelled up his thin frame to his torn denim shirt. His face was as white as his hands, but for a shadow on his jutting chin. His cheeks were thin to hollowness; his mouth was wide; there were shallow, almost delicate indentations at his temples, and his gray eyes were so colourless I thought he was blind. His hair was dead and thin, almost feathery on top of his head.

> **Slow movement** of Scout's gaze takes in the character's clothing and face. 'Gray' eyes and 'dead' hair makes us wonder if she is seeing a ghost or some supernatural monster.

Emotion pervades as the character gradually relaxes 'into a timid smile' and Scout begins to cry.

When I pointed to him his palms slipped slightly, leaving greasy sweat streaks on the wall, and he hooked his thumbs in his belt. A strange small spasm shook him, as if he heard fingernails scrape slate, but as I gazed at him in wonder the tension slowly drained from his face. His lips parted into a timid smile, and our neighbor's image blurred with my sudden tears.

Finally the **epiphany** as the mystery man is revealed as Boo Radley. The reader has waited like Scout for a very long time to see him, and when we do he is the **courageous hero**.

'Hey, Boo,' I said.

key point

Revise two prescribed **novels** and at least one **short story**.

exam Q

Exam Question 2017 (SEC Junior Cycle Sample 3)

Section C – Reading Comprehension Strategies – Our World

6,755,987,239
WORLD POPULATION

1 SEC.
4.3 BIRTHS
1.8 DEATHS

LIFE EXPECTANCY
(HI) 84.36 MACAU
(LO) 31.88 SWAZILAND

BIRTHS PER WOMAN
(HI) 7.34 MALI
(LO) 0.9 MACAU

CHINA 19.62%
Nearly one out of five people in the world live in China.

INDIA 17.25%
India is one-third the size of the US, yet has nearly four times more people.

UNITED STATES 4.53%
The US ranks third in both population and in land mass.

INDONESIA 3.40%
Indonesia is made up of over 17,000 islands of which roughly 6,000 are inhabited.

BRAZIL 2.82%
Brazil occupies the fifth largest land area in the world and the third largest in the Americas.

Question 1   5 marks

Study the above infographic on world population carefully, then complete the following sentences using only the information provided.

(a) The country with the greatest number of people living in it is:

_____

(b) The birth rate per woman in the Republic of Ireland is 2.01. A country on the infographic with a birth rate more than three times the rate in the Republic of Ireland is:_____

(c) A country referred to in the infographic with a low average life expectancy is:

_____

(d) The infographic suggests that, overall, the population of the world is decreasing.
Write either T for true or F for false in the box provided.

(e) India is more densely populated than the United States.
Write either T for true or F for false in the box provided.

Study the screenshot from a White House blog below and answer the following questions.

| *the* **WHITE HOUSE** PRESIDENT BARACK OBAMA | BRIEFING ROOM | ISSUES | THE ADMINISTRATION | 1600 PENN | |

HOME · BLOG

Bringing Our Immigration System into the Digital Age

JULY 15, 2015 AT 3:00 PM ET BY CECILIA MUÑOZ, MIKEY DICKERSON

Summary: Federal agencies are undertaking new actions to improve the visa experience for families, workers, employers, and people in need of humanitarian relief.

In November, President Obama announced a series of Executive Actions to fix the broken immigration system. As a part of these efforts, he charged the key federal agencies responsible for administering our legal immigration system to explore ways to modernize and streamline the system. The goal was to develop recommendations to bring the system into the 21st century to grow our economy, help businesses and workers, and protect families.

Today, we are taking the next step in this effort, releasing a report on Modernizing and Streamlining Our Legal Immigration System for the 21st Century. This report includes a wide range of new actions that federal agencies will undertake to improve the visa experience for families, workers, employers, and people in need of humanitarian relief.

Question 2   5 marks

(a) Identify two digital elements used in the above blog.

Digital element 1: _____

Digital element 2: _____

(b) How can the use of digital elements, like the ones you have identified above, lead to more effective communication of information? You may refer to the above blog and/or other sources in your answer.

Question 3   *10 marks*

The Department of Foreign Affairs is holding a competition inviting secondary school students to devise two guidelines that will help newly arrived immigrants adjust to living in Ireland.

It is intended that the guidelines will be printed on government publications like information leaflets and posters.

In the spaces provided, clearly state each guideline. Suggest an image that would be appropriate to accompany each guideline. Give a reason for both your choice of guideline and its accompanying image.

Guideline (a): _____

_____

_____

Image: _____

_____

_____

Reason: _____

_____

_____

Guideline (b): _____

_____

_____

Image: _____

_____

_____

Reason: _____

_____

_____

Additional Writing Space. Label all work clearly with the question number and part.

_____

_____

_____

_____

_____

_____

_____

_____

_____

_____

_____

5 Different Ways of Writing: Engaging in the Writing Process

In this section you will revise writing for a number of different purposes. You will:

- **Read** a number of **samples** of different **styles** of writing.
- **Learn** how to identify the **purpose** of a writing **task**.
- **Match** the **audience** for a piece of writing with a suitable **register**.
- **Practise planning** answers to give your writing **structure**.
- **Explore techniques** for **composing** fresh and original texts of your own.
- **Analyse** sample **questions, hints and answers**.

Every time we use a pen and paper to **write**, we are **aiming to communicate a message** to an individual or group using **words** that will **connect** with that **audience**. The same is equally true for every **text, instant message** or **email** composed. The great English author E.M. Forster captured this succinctly when he advised all young writers to **'Only connect!'** The main **purpose** of all writing is to reach your intended **audience**.

Writing style is crucial for all good **communication**. It is also vital, however, to connect with your reader by selecting **appropriately memorable content** to write about. Deciding **what material** to explore and **how to express yourself** is the focus for this unit.

Think of yourself as a **writer** who possesses a number of **writing skill sets**. Your aim is to **develop** your ability to write **fiction** and **non-fiction** in a wide **variety** of **genres**. The measure of **success** is always the same: **are you connecting** with the person reading your work?

- **Purpose = What** you are asked to write.
- **Audience = Who** you are writing to/for.
- **Register = How** you express your ideas.

L.O. W 3

Write for a variety of purposes, for example to:

- analyse
- evaluate
- imagine
- explore, etc.

Types of questions

In the Junior Cycle exam, writing for different purposes can be tested with different types of questions:

1. Writing **instructions** – a list of **clear steps** explaining **how** to perform a task successfully.
2. Writing **blogs** – **personal web pages** written in an **informal** or **conversational style**.
3. Writing **personal letters** – **intimate** written messages to **family** or **close friends**.
4. Writing **dialogue** – a fictional **conversation** between two or more characters.
5. Writing **interviews** – conversations where **questions** are asked and **answers** are given.
6. Writing a **podcast/short talk** for radio/writing a **focused discussion** of a topic broadcast on talk radio.

Suitable vocabulary

Thinking about your writing involves **understanding** and **learning suitable vocabulary** used in questions about writing. The following table includes **key terms** you will need to know in order to write well.

Clarity	Writing where the meaning of words and sentences is easily understood.
Imperative	The command form of a verb used when giving orders or instructions.
Logic	A proper or reasonable way of thinking about or understanding something.
Numbered	Using numbers in a list to indicate a sequence of steps or points.
Syntax	The sequence in which words are put together to form sentences.
Task	A specific situation with a clear writing purpose or aim.

Writing guidelines or instructions

You may be asked to write a **set** of **instructions** or a **list** of **guidelines**. The essence of giving good instructions is that they follow a **clear** and **logical sequence**. You must think about the task and make sure the points you write follow the **correct order**.

Imagine you were asked to **give directions** for someone to drive from your school to your home. The instructions must begin in one location and **outline step-by-step** the route that must be taken to arrive at the correct destination. Take ten minutes to write out the directions to your house. Try to limit the directions to **short sentences** and if possible limit the instructions to **ten points**. Each point should be **numbered** and begin with a **verb in the imperative** or **command** form. The following example illustrates these points:

1. **Turn** left at the main school gates on to College Road.
2. **Drive** for .5 of a kilometre to the Callan roundabout.
3. **Take** the first exit from the roundabout and follow the sign for 'Kells'.

Now write your own set of directions. Make sure you write in a **simple** and **direct** style. The points should be **short** and follow a **logical sequence**.

A set of guidelines resembles instructions, as you are recommending a **course of action** or a **series of steps** to be taken in order to **complete** a **task** or fulfil certain conditions.

1. **Clarity** is paramount here so your points should be numbered.
2. They should be expressed as **commands** in the **imperative mode**.
3. **Sentences** should be **brief** and **precise**.

You will be awarded high marks for writing guidelines or instructions following this style.

Sample question and answer

Question 1   25 marks

Write a list of safety guidelines to be displayed on a poster EITHER in your school's Science lab OR in the Technology, Woodwork, Metalwork or Home Economics room.

Allow 15 minutes for 25-mark questions.

Sample answer

Laboratory Rules for Pupils

1. **DO NOT** enter the **laboratory** without **permission**.
2. **DO NOT** use any **equipment** unless **permitted** to do so by the **teacher**. Make sure you know exactly what you are supposed to do. If in doubt, **ask** the **teacher**.
3. Long hair **MUST** always be tied back securely.
4. **ALWAYS** wear eye protection when instructed to do so.
5. **ALWAYS** check that the label on the bottle is **EXACTLY** the same as the material you require. If in doubt, ask the teacher.
6. **NOTHING** must be tasted, eaten or drunk in the laboratory.
7. Any substance accidentally taken into the mouth must be spat out **IMMEDIATELY** and the mouth washed out with plenty of water. The **incident** must be **reported** to the **teacher**.
8. Any **cut, burn** or other accident **MUST** be reported at once to the teacher.
9. Any chemicals spilled on the skin or clothing **MUST** be washed at once with plenty of water and reported to the teacher.
10. **ALWAYS WASH** your hands after practical work.

Composing a blog

The word 'blog' is short for 'web-log'. A **log** is another word for a journal or diary, and the world wide **web** is the revolutionary modern method of mass communication. Once the internet became accessible to millions of users, the number of blogs grew dramatically. Celebrity blogs and video blogs have generated a huge audience among young adults.

All blogs have the following characteristics:

- Regularly **updated** website.
- **Personal** journal or diary.
- **Comment** and opinions.
- **Multi media** – graphics, text, audio, video.
- **Newest** posts at the top.

 **L.O. W 4**

Write competently in a range of text forms, for example:
- letter
- report
- multi-modal text
- review
- blog

using appropriate vocabulary, tone and a variety of styles to achieve a chosen purpose for different audiences.

key point

The **target audience** for any broadcast or publication is the **specific group** of people it is aimed at addressing.

Blogs are a very efficient way of reaching an audience. They offer readers a forum in which to **interact** with the writer. Blogs are a **form** of writing that can be **accessed** at home or work on a **computer**, and when you are on the move by means of a **smartphone** or **tablet**. This ease of access means that blogs are **frequently refreshed** and updated. Readers can find out about the **blogger's life** and **opinions** and also keep track of other **readers' comments** online.

Suitable vocabulary

Blogs are **web pages**, so when you discuss websites you must use the **correct words** to identify **typical features**. Learn the vocabulary on the following page and use it to **demonstrate your knowledge** of how websites work.

Banner	Graphic image announcing name of a site or an advertisement for a site.
Biog.	Short outline of author's professional life.
Colour scheme	An arrangement of colours and tones designed to appeal to viewers.
Headers	Main navigation bar at the top of a web page.
Links	Connections to other websites – short for 'hyperlinks'.
Logos	A symbol representing a brand or company.
Posts	Content web pages in reverse chronological order.
Sidebars	A shorter piece of text that accompanies a longer article.

Sample question and hints

Question 1

Read the screenshot below of a blog post by Carrie Hope Fletcher and answer the questions which follow. Carrie is a celebrity actress, songwriter and novelist whose blog and video blog regularly reach an audience of millions.

Carrie Hope Fletcher

My Name is Carrie Hope Fletcher. I am an Actress/Singer/Songwriter, author of Sunday Times Bestsellers 'All I Know Now' and 'On the Other Side' and 'All That She Can See'. Hope you like my blog and if you have any questions… Ask Away!

FAQ

Random Archive Ask me anything

Follow carriehopefletcher | tumblr.

<3

Public relationships are a weird thing. No one has an entitlement to anything within them but once one thing has been shared, it's hard to know where the line is between what anyone other than you or your partner should/shouldn't know. What I do know though is that if that relationship comes to an end, it's hard to avoid telling people whether they have a right to know or not. Given the amount of questions I've already had, the longer I leave it, the worse it could be for all involved. So…here goes.

Pete and I broke up.

A couple of months ago.

It's so much easier to explain a break up when something…happens. When someone lies, cheats, uses, abuses or even falls for someone else and you can say that's why. That's why we broke up. But in this case, nothing went wrong. We just simply weren't right.

That's really all I can and want to say on it all. Pete and I are still friends, of course. We shared two and a half incredibly magic years together, we both taught each other a lot and we'll continue to be in each other's lives until the end.

I just ask that you don't ask questions and you don't do the whole "OH BUT WHHHYYYY?! YOU WERE SO PERFECT FOR EACH OTHER!!!"…because who does that help, really? We both appreciate that in any public relationship, especially a "youtube" relationship everyone feels very *involved* but only two people were involved in our relationship: myself and Pete and we'd appreciate it if everyone could respect that. We're both okay and moving forwards and that's the main thing.

Much, MUCH love and thanks.

<3

a) State whether you think the following statements are true or false based on your reading of this blog page.

Statement	TRUE	FALSE
The author is a film star.		✓
She has just broken up with her boyfriend.	✓	
The relationship ended because he cheated on her.		✓
Carrie and Pete are still good friends.	✓	
The author wants readers to respect their need for privacy.	✓	

b) How well does this web page inform us about the author, Carrie?

Hint: b)
Evaluate the quality of the page, discussing how key facts about her are presented.

c) Do you agree that the language is suitable for a personal blog post? Explain your answer.

Hint: c)
Is the language and syntax accessible, formal, informal, colloquial, technical or personal?

d) Comment on the design and layout. Is it appealing to the viewers?

Hint: d)
Look at the banner, colour scheme, use of graphics, logos and sidebars.

e) Write a web post for a day in the life of a celebrity. The subject for your blog could be:

- A famous mixed martial arts fighter.
- A TV chat show host.
- The star of a soap opera or situation comedy.
- A Premier League football player.
- A model contestant in a reality TV show.

Hints: e)
- Make sure the post is **written** in the **first person**.
- Keep the **content fresh**, immediate and up to date.
- Use **short, clear sentences**.
- **Use an intimate** personal tone.

Writing a personal letter

Personal letters, which are letters written to close family members, lovers and friends will always be composed in a casual and intimate style.

- The **language** should be **informal**.
- The **content** will reflect the **close nature** of the **relationship**.
- **Your address** should appear in the **top right-hand corner** of the page followed by the **date**.
- The **greeting** should be appropriately **casual or friendly** and is followed by a comma.
- Begin the **body of the letter** on the next line directly beneath this comma.
- Each **new idea** or subject means a **new paragraph**.
- Your **closing salutation** will be **affectionate** and **casual**.

The following template illustrates the layout of a personal letter.

Your Address
Your Address

Today's date

Familiar greeting,

Body of the letter – one idea, one paragraph

Body of the letter – one idea, one paragraph

Body of the letter – one idea, one paragraph

Intimate closing phrase,

Your signature.

Letter to my eight-year-old self

Personal letters are traditionally addressed to **close family members** and **intimate friends**. It is a **genre** where we typically communicate our most **personal thoughts** and **feelings** to an audience we **trust**.

One interesting **development** of this method of writing is to write a **personal letter** to **yourself**. Many people have used this **technique** to **explore** their vision for their career by writing to their **future self**. The personal letter becomes a means of **expressing dreams** and **ambitions** we hope to fulfil later in life.

On the other hand, a letter to my **younger self** allows an adult or older person to **reflect** on their **childhood** with the benefit of **hindsight**. It is a way of **making sense** of the **past** from the **point of view** of the **present** moment. It has been used to great effect by many **celebrities** from the world of music, cinema and sport.

Check out the famous Brazilian footballer Ronaldinho's 'Letter to my eight-year-old-self' on The Players' Tribute website at

www.theplayerstribune.com/en-us/articles/letter-to-my-younger-self-ronaldinho

 L.O. W 9

Engage in the writing process as a private, pleasurable and purposeful activity, and using a personal voice as individual style is thoughtfully developed.

Sample question and answer

Question 1   *30 marks*

Using Ronaldinho's letter as a model, write a letter to your eight-year-old self.

Allow 20 minutes for 30-mark questions.

High marks are awarded for:

- **Original** material
- Correct **layout**
- **Suitable** vocabulary
- **Clear** writing

Sample answer

20/2/2017

Dear eight-year-old Jim,

You'll be coming home from school on a cold day in January. It will be snowing very hard. You will open the door and smell the hot stew Mam already has on the table. You will walk off for ten minutes to let it cool before eating it. You'll be glad it's Friday and that you have no homework.

After looking at telly for two hours, you will return to the kitchen. Dad has just walked in the door. You are hopeful that a dog will follow him because you have been asking for one. Your heart will sink when he tells you that he has only enquired about the dog. You will start to complain loudly, when suddenly you hear a whimper, you look down at the floor and see a Jack Russell pup with brown patches looking up at you from big, sad eyes. You will run over to him and rub him, but not too roughly or you might scare him off. The dog will seem distracted, not lapping up any of the attention.

After a week you're going to name him Tayto, because he seems to like eating them. You will start to take him on walks, even bringing him up to the school. Unfortunately, he will hop out of the car and run right in front of another vehicle. Luckily it will stop just in time.

Later on, you will find him chewing on rats, mice, cats, hares, rabbits and even your slippers. He will earn a reputation for eating absolutely everything. However, you will come downstairs one day and find him unable to do anything. You will later find out that he was chewing on poisonous berries from a bush in your garden.

The vet will tell you that the mortality rate from the plant's berries, *Deadly Nightshade*, is very high, 97%. He will probably go into respiratory failure and pass gently away. You will take Tayto home for more than likely his last living day.

You will wake up the following morning and come downstairs in a state of anxiety. To your surprise, Tayto will be there wagging his tail. The vet will call him a fighter, just like what all Jack Russells are known for. He will marvel at his struggle, with only a 3% chance of survival. But Tayto will show his courage, every single time, he'd just fight for that sliver of hope, showing that 'death won't get me' attitude.

Later again, as an older dog, he will tone it down a little. He will still have that one important thing though, a lively, beating heart.

So now, what will you learn from all this? Are you going to be the ninety-seven-point-five percent that play it safe, roll over to die?

Or are you going to fight?

Yours truly,

Jim Kirby

EXAMINER'S COMMENT

- Suitable **structure** and **form** for a **personal** letter.
- **Dramatic personal** account of a boy's first pet.
- Well **modelled** on Ronaldinho's letter.

MARKS AWARDED: Ex: 30/28 (90–100%) Distinction

 **L.O. W 4**

Write competently in a range of text forms, for example:
- letter
- report
- multi-modal text
- review
- blog

using appropriate vocabulary, tone and a variety of styles to achieve a chosen purpose for different audiences.

Dialogues/scripts/screenplays

Writing **dialogue** is a skill you will need to develop for your Junior Cycle exam. Dialogue is what we call the **words spoken** by fictional characters. Dialogue can appear in **short stories, novels** and **poems**, as well as in **scripts** for drama and in film **screenplays**. Important features of dialogue to keep in mind are:

- **Vocabulary** suitable to the character's personality and background.
- Realistic **conversational style**.
- **Format** includes **character's name** in the **left-hand margin** followed by a **colon**.
- **Dramatic content** makes the scene **memorable**.

Sample question and hints

Question 1

Read the following scene from the drama *Private Peaceful* by Michael Morpurgo and answer the questions which follow.

The background

In this extract two brothers, Tommo and Charlie Peaceful, are part of an English regiment fighting in the trenches of World War I. Although both brothers have been injured their Commanding Officer, Sergeant Hanley, expects them to fight on with the rest of the troops.

Charlie: Thought we'd lost you, Tommo. The same shell that buried you killed half a dozen of the others. You were lucky. Your head looks a bit of a mess, though. Me, I can't feel my legs. I think I've lost a lot of blood.

Tommo: Where are we, Charlie?

Charlie: Middle of bloody no-man's-land, that's where, some old German dug-out.

Tommo: We'd best stay here for a while, hadn't we, Charlie?

Sergeant Hanley: Stay put? Stay put? You're worse than your brother, Peaceful. Our orders are to press home the attack and then hold our ground. Only fifty yards or so to the German trenches. On your feet, all of you.

(No one moves.)

Sergeant Hanley: What in hell's name is the matter with you lot? On your feet, damn you! On your feet!

Tommo: I think we are all thinking the same thing, Sergeant. You take us out there now and the machine guns will mow us down. Maybe we should stay here and then go back later when it gets dark? No point in going out there and getting ourselves killed for nothing, is there Sergeant?

Sergeant Hanley: Are you disobeying my order, Private Peaceful?

Tommo: No, I'm just letting you know what I think. What we all think.

Sergeant Hanley: And I'm telling you, Peaceful, that if you don't come with us when we go, it'll be a court martial for you. It'll be the firing squad. Do you hear me, Peaceful?

Do you hear me?

A. For each of the questions below tick the correct box.

> **L.O. R 1**
>
> Read texts with fluency, understanding and competence, decoding groups of words/phrases and not just single words.

  a) This scene from the play is set in:

  i. A schoolroom ☐

  ii. A battlefield ☑

  iii. A courtroom ☐

  b) There is conflict between:

  i. Hanley and Charlie ☐

  ii. Charlie and Tommo ☐

  iii. Tommo and Hanley ☑

  c) The style of language in the dialogue is:

  i. Formal ☐

  ii. Colloquial ☑

  iii. Poetic ☐

B. Radio is sometimes referred to as 'Theatre of the Mind'.

  If you were in charge of producing *Private Peaceful*, would you prefer to put it on as:

  1. A live stage play

  2. A radio play/podcast

  3. A feature film in the cinema?

  Explain why.

> ### Hint
> This drama question requires you to display a knowledge of the technical challenges of **staging a play**, recording a **radio performance** or **shooting** a **scene** for a **film**. Your answer should refer to some of the following:
>
> - Lighting
> - Sound effects
> - Actors
> - Costumes
> - Props
> - Sets
>
>
>
> Focused **knowledge of stagecraft** will earn you high marks in the exam.

C. Hanley issues Tommo with an ultimatum, 'if you don't come with us when we go, it'll be a court martial for you.' Write a **short dialogue** where a soldier is **cross examined** during a **court martial** because he/she is accused of **disobeying an order**.

> ### Hint
> **Format** your **dialogue** with **characters' names** in the left-hand **margin** indicating which lines they speak. Try to imitate the **style of language** used by the characters above. You will also have to **invent new characters** and include their spoken lines of dialogue. It is a good idea to include one or two **stage directions** like the one mentioned on the previous page '(no one moves)'. Make sure the **action** is **dramatic**!

Interviews

Interviews are **similar** to **dialogue** because both share the same **format**. The structure of all interviews is to **alternate questions** and **answers**. The **interviewer's name** will appear in the **left-hand margin**, followed by a **colon** and a **question** or **comment**. Standard practice is to write out the **interviewee's name below** this and include his or her **answer** to the question. It is a **formal** way of presenting a **structured conversation** between two people.

Interviews can appear on **television**, on **radio, online** as a YouTube **video** or in **print** form in a **magazine** or **newspaper**. As readers or viewers, we seem to have an insatiable appetite for finding out about the **private lives, thoughts** and **opinions** of our **heroes**. Think of memorable interviews with **celebrity singers, actors** or **sports stars**. One crucial aspect of the media industry is covering and broadcasting **exclusive** intimate interviews with public figures.

Sample question and hints

Question 1

Imagine you were a guest on a TV or radio talk show. Write the text of the interview where you discuss an important moment from your childhood. You might like to choose one of the following:

- A visit to the doctor, dentist or hospital accident and emergency room.
- Meeting someone again after a long time.
- A stroke of luck.
- You and your friends were caught doing something wrong and got in trouble.
- Something unexpected happened and you had to act quickly.
- You are given a grown-up job to do for the first time.
- Someone is kind to you at a difficult time in your life.

Hints:

- Think about the **kinds** of **questions** someone might ask about this incident.
- Break the story into **at least three parts**: beginning, middle and end.
- Write about how the event made an **impact** on you **at the time**.
- Finally, you can talk about **how you make sense** of it **now** as an older teenager.
- Use the **structure** of Ryan's interview with Emmet as a **model** for your answer.

 L.O. W 7

Respond imaginatively in writing to texts, showing a critical appreciation of:

- language
- style and content
- choice of words
- language patterns
- tone
- images

Podcasts/short talks for radio

Podcasts are **audio** or **video** clips hosted on a website. The advantage of keeping these highlights online is that listeners or viewers who miss a programme can **stream** or **download** it later. Podcasting has changed the way we **access content**. Instead of listening live or recording a programme, the content is available for us to enjoy at any time that is most convenient.

The key difference between an interview and a short talk for the radio is that instead of two voices, interviewer and interviewee, the listeners only hear a single voice. The content of a talk could be:

- A hobby or pastime you enjoy.
- What it means to be a member of your local club.

- A significant moment in your life and how it affected you.
- Someone you admire or look up to as a role model.

Sample question and answer

Question 1   50 marks

Write a short talk for your local radio station where you talk about the journey of a lifetime. You may discuss a real journey you have already taken or write about a trip you would like to take at some point in the future.

Allow 30 minutes for 50-mark questions.

Sample answer

Making a Difference

By Padraic Mullen

Let me tell you all about the most interesting place I have ever been. Cape Town in South Africa. I got there on a nice bright sunny day two years ago. The landscape was very rough with cacti and palm trees nearly everywhere I looked.

L.O. W 11

Use language conventions appropriately, especially punctuation and spelling, to aid meaning and presentation, and to enhance the reader's experience.

The volunteers and I stepped off of the plane and felt every bit of the 30 degree heat. Sweat started pouring from my forehead as soon as I stepped on the runway. We were in the main airport in Cape Town, a huge modern building. It took us about 30 minutes to get through security and collect our bags. When we had picked up the luggage we left the airport and went outside to get a taxi to the hotel.

The minute we turned into the driveway of the *Sensation Heights* hotel we knew it was going to be magnificent. Picture the scene; beautiful bushes, trees, flowers all greener than anything you have ever seen. A spectacular fountain jetting water high above a deep blue pond just outside the gleaming glass doors where we got dropped off.

The porter came and took our bags up to our room as we checked in at the big reception area. I saw a glittering chandelier. There was cool marble everywhere and we were given complimentary drinks. So far it was top class treatment.

We went up to our room and got a shower to get rid of the jet lag. We were back down in the lobby 30 minutes later. We took a taxi heading for the slums where we would be working for the next week. You could feel the excitement in the car on the way.

When we got there it was a shock to the system. Everyone just stopped, looked around and took it all in. It was like nothing we had ever expected. The way these people had been living was just not right. It showed how different our lives are to theirs, how well off we are. The shacks were thrown together with anything they could find. Scraps of tin, plastic, anything. They had no food, all starving and could do nothing. Young boys and girls were wearing rags way too small for them.

Listeners, I mean no disrespect to the people living there, but the smell was unbearable. They just went to the toilet wherever they could get enough privacy. There could have been maybe 10 people living in a small tin shack half the size of my bedroom. I don't know how anyone could ever live like that.

I left there that day a different man, determined to help these people live a half decent life. The next day we got up at 6 in the morning and went to the building site. It was a real challenge getting up so early but we were all determined to do our best to help out. We had great fun, don't get me wrong, the craic was mighty but we had one goal! Make these people's lives change forever.

We set off that day and never looked back for the rest of the week. It was amazing just being there. We built 165 houses in the week between just 480 volunteers. It was phenomenal how many houses were built that week. The determination of the group was at an all-time high and we made a real difference.

Handing over the first house for me was by far the greatest moment of the trip. Looking into that women's eyes and seeing the joy. Getting the chance to change the lives of her children and herself took my breath away. Just the emotion in her face at that moment in time was something that I will never forget as long as I live.

I think you will understand when I say that this experience is one I will never forget. I made so many friends on the site while building the houses, some have become friends for life. But by far the greatest thing was giving these people a sense of hope that they can have a good life. Not being worried about if their house was going to blow away overnight. Now because of that week those people will always have a roof over their heads and can live long, happy lives together. The legacy of that trip will live on in their lives forever. The journey of a lifetime in many ways.

> **L.O. W 10**
>
> Use and apply knowledge of language structures, for example
> - sentence structure
> - paragraphing
> - grammar
>
> to make writing a richer experience.

EXAMINER'S COMMENT

- **Personal** memory is **dramatic**.
- Strong **emotion** is evoked.
- **Contrasting images** of wealth and poverty are given.
- **Colloquial** language and **authentic voice**.

MARKS AWARDED: **Ex: 50/40** (90–100%) Distinction

Exam Question 2017 (Junior Cycle 2017, Final Examination, English Higher Level)

Section D – Engaging in the Writing Process

Question 1   *25 marks*

Study the word cloud printed below. Complete the task that follows.

Why can't you be like...?
Wet towel pile on bathroom floor Up all night, in bed all day
"There's never anything to eat in this house" Storming out of the room
You're a complete Mystery to me
You're not going out wearing that YOU JUST MMS (Major Mood Swing) DON'T GET IT
"Everyone else is going ..."
Yeah Right Whatever "You just don't understand me"
How could you? Totally empty fridge – again Door Slam
Your room is a pig sty! SO embarrassing!
Cheeky Grunt Mouldy plates and mugs in bedroom
Facebook activity at 3 am Used up all the hot water
Texting at the table Barefaced lie Eye Roll
Shoes EVERYWHERE "I hate you"
Compulsive selfie taking Treat this place like a hotel
Every single light in the house switched on and left on
Totally silent car journey involving headphone use
Overflowing laundry basket

Using one or more of the words or phrases from the word cloud above, write the dialogue for a scene in a TV drama where an adult confronts a teenager *or a* teenager confronts an adult. Your dialogue may be serious or humorous or both. You may refer to location, the use of special effects and make suggestions for movement in your script. Indicate each speaker on the left-hand side of the page.

_____

_____

_____

_____

_____

_____

6 Responding to Stories: Unseen and Studied Fiction

In this section you will revise **reading** and **writing** about **fictional texts** in a number of ways:

- **Analyse** typical **methods** of **creating** fictional **characters**.
- **Read** and **compare** several **opening moments** from **young adult novels**.
- **Learn** how to **explain** the **importance** of the **narrator** in fiction.
- **Respond** to and write about **fiction** using **appropriate language**.
- Select **key moments** and **make judgements** about **character** and **mood**.
- Discuss how an author's **choice of words** and use of **imagery** can **enrich fiction**.
- **Analyse** sample **questions, hints** and **answers**.

Few of us can resist the **lure** of a **good story**. From the magical realms of the **children's fairytale** to the fascination of **celebrity gossip**, we spend much of our lives **engaging** with **compelling narratives**. **Fictional stories** feature in the Junior Cycle in many forms, from **short stories** to **novels** and **feature films**. In this section we will revise **unseen** and **studied prose fiction**. You will look again at the **key elements** of **storytelling** in **short fiction** and **novels**. You will **practise** the **skills** of **analysing** and **responding critically** to a number of different **unseen narrative extracts**.

 L.O. R 6

Read texts for understanding and appreciation of character, setting, story and action:

- to explore how and why characters develop
- to recognise the importance of setting and plot structure

Finally, you will revise the **key features** of the **novels** and **short stories** you have **studied**. A vital step in your preparation for the Junior Cycle exam is to **draw together** your **knowledge** of your **studied stories** so that you can **discuss** them in a **well-informed** and **critical** manner.

Creating an interesting opening moment in fiction

Storytellers use a powerful **metaphor** to illustrate the **irresistible attraction** of a strong **opening moment** in a story. The best short stories and novels **'hook'** the reader at the start so that we are like fish **captivated** by something that has **power** over us. Our curiosity is so intense that we are **drawn** into the **fictional world** because we **care deeply** about the **characters** and their **fate**.

Good writers **create situations** and **characters** from the **initial paragraph**s, forcing us to **read** on. The following are some of the **typical features** of interesting opening **scenes** in fiction. **Learn** the **meaning** of each one of these key terms and **practise** the skill of **recognising** and **explaining** their **effectiveness** in fiction.

Analyse fiction using **suitable language** in the correct way.

Characterisation	Building a fictional character, giving details of their appearance, behaviour and thoughts.
Dialogue	Using a character's speech to reveal emotion or create tension.
Imagery	Putting pictures in the reader's mind by supplying precise detail.
Language	Using vocabulary and syntax to create a tone and mood for the story.
Mystery	Deliberately creating an atmosphere of intense uncertainty by omitting detail.
Originality	Avoiding cliché – making characters and situations seem fresh and unique.
Setting	Suggesting the world of the story in description of physical location and mood.
Suspense	Keeping the reader waiting to find out some key information crucial to the plot.

Young adult fiction

One of the most **popular genres** of storytelling is 'young adult' fiction. **Teenage readers** eager to immerse themselves in the stories of **young protagonists** are turning to these books in ever-increasing numbers.

The **unseen fiction** questions focus on **reading** and **responding** in order to discover the power of a **good opening** page to 'hook' the reader.

- Always **read** the **question** carefully.
- Answer the **full** question.

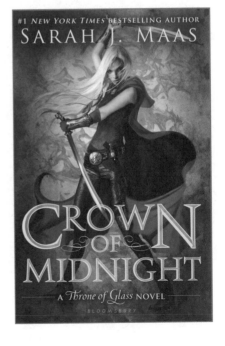

Sample questions and answers

Read the **opening paragraphs** of *Crown of Midnight* by Sarah J. Maas and the **sample questions** and **answers** which follow.

The shutters swinging in the storm winds were the only sign of her entry. No one had noticed her scaling the garden wall of the darkened manor house, and with the thunder and the gusting wind off the nearby sea, no one heard her as she shimmied up the drainpipe, swung onto the windowsill, and slithered into the second-floor hallway.

The King's Champion pressed herself into an alcove at the thud of approaching steps. Concealed beneath a black mask and hood, she willed herself to melt into the shadows, to become nothing more than a slip of darkness. A servant girl trudged past to the open window, grumbling as she latched it shut. Seconds later, she disappeared down the stairwell at the other end of the hall. The girl hadn't noticed the wet footprints on the floorboards.

Lightning flashed, illuminating the hallway. The assassin took a long breath, going over the plans she'd painstakingly memorised in the three days she'd been watching the manor house on the outskirts of Bellhaven. Five doors on each side. Lord Nirall's bedroom was the third on the left.

She listened for the approach of any other servants, but the house remained hushed as the storm raged around them.

Question 1

In the case of each of the following, write the letter corresponding to the correct answer in the appropriate box.

(a) Which word best describes the **central character's movements** in the first paragraph:

A. nimble

B. stealthy ✓

C. quick

(b) In **contrast**, the character of the **servant girl** in the second paragraph is:

A. lazy

B. awkward

C. careless ✓

(c) Based on what you have read in this passage, which **adjective** best describes the **mood**:

A. ominous ✓

B. sad

C. comical

L.O. **R 11**

Comment on the use of language features in stories and explain what makes them effective.

Question 2   20 marks

Show how this writer's **choice of words** creates a **compelling scene** to **hook** the reader.

Sample answer

Point 1: In the opening paragraph, **energetic verbs** are used to introduce us to an **exciting scenario**. First of all, the **'swinging'** shutters are the only sign the assassin has gained entry. Other **verbs** used to describe the **motion** of the **intruder** are **'scaling' 'slithered' 'swung'** and **'shimmied'**. This variety of **dynamic** action words combines to communicate the hero's **skill, agility** and **furtiveness**. The **central character** is **introduced** through an **expert clandestine incursion** into **enemy territory**. This is the first way the author's **vocabulary establishes** a **tense scene** to capture our attention.

Allow 12 minutes for 20-mark questions.

Point 2: The writer, Sarah J. Maas, cleverly **contrasts** the **subterfuge** of the 'King's Champion' with the **carelessness** of Lord Nirall's maid. **'No one noticed'** the entrance of the **masked killer**, whereas the **'approaching steps'** of the **servant** announce her arrival with the **onomatopoeia** of words like **'thud'** and **'trudged'**. This choice of **words** to **emphasise sound** draws the reader into the scene and develops with the use of the verb **'grumbling'** to suggest a noisy servant who resents this interruption to her night-time routine. Her **failure** to notice the signs of an intruder further **highlights** the **cunning guile** of the assassin, making the reader even more curious about the **mysterious** trespasser.

 **L.O. W 7**

Respond imaginatively in writing to texts, showing a critical appreciation of:

* language
* style and content.
* choice of words
* language patterns
* tone
* images

EXAMINER'S COMMENT

* Sharp **focus** on the question combines well with higher-order **analysis** of the writer's **style**.
* Answer is **expressed fluently** in a **formal register** suited to **critical discussion** of a text.
* Candidate **develops ideas** in depth and uses **suitable supporting material** accurately.

MARKS AWARDED: Ex. 20/19 (90–100%) Distinction

Comparing extracts from two different novels

A similar style of Junior Cycle question will require you to **read** and **compare** two passages from **different novels** or **short stories**. When you are asked to **compare**, you must look for **both similarities** and **differences** between the extracts.

 **L.O. R 2**

Read for a variety of purposes:
- learning
- pleasure
- research
- comparison

Sample question and hints

Compare the **characterisation** in the **opening pages** of the **novels** *Artemis Fowl* and *Reckless*.

Artemis Fowl
By Eoin Colfer

How does one describe Artemis Fowl? Various psychiatrists have tried and failed. The main problem is Artemis's own intelligence. He bamboozles every test thrown at him. He has puzzled the greatest medical minds and sent many of them gibbering to their own hospitals.

There is no doubt that Artemis is a child prodigy. But why does someone of such brilliance dedicate himself to criminal activities? This is a question that can be answered by only one person. And he delights in not talking.

Perhaps the best way to create an accurate picture of Artemis is to tell the by now famous account of his first villainous venture. I have put together this report from first-hand interviews with the victims, and as the tale unfolds you will realise that this was not easy.

Reckless
By Cornelia Funke

Once upon a time.

The night breathed through the apartment like a dark animal. The ticking of a clock. The groan of a floorboard as he slipped out of his room. All was drowned by its silence. But Jacob loved the night. He felt it on his skin like a promise. Like a cloak woven from freedom and danger.

Outside the stars were paled by the glaring lights of the city, and the large apartment was stale with his mother's sorrow. She did not wake as he stole into her room, even when he carefully opened the drawer of her bedside table. The key lay right next to the pills that let her sleep. Its cool metal nestled in his hand as he stepped back out into the dark corridor.

There was still a light burning in his brother's room – Will was afraid of the dark – and Jacob made sure he was fast asleep before unlocking the door to their father's study. Their mother had not entered there since his disappearance, but for Jacob this was not the first time he had sneaked into the empty room to search for the answers she did not want to give.

Hints

- **Both** stories **focus** on the **central character immediately**. The first paragraph of *Artemis Fowl* focuses on the **protagonist's** extraordinary **intellect** and ability to confound the experts.

- In **both narratives**, the central **character's intelligence** is **emphasised**.

- 'Jacob', the hero of *Reckless*, is also a clever individual but here his **skill** at **eluding detection** is **hinted** at rather than explicitly stated.

- The **narrator** of *Artemis Fowl* **arouses** our **curiosity** about the **main character** by asking **two key questions**. The **first implies** that the **individual** is **exceptional** and **defies description**. The **second introduces** the idea that Artemis devotes his **prodigious intellect** to a life of **crime** of which the **narrator** has **expert** knowledge.

- In *Reckless*, the **main figure** is **introduced** by means of a **third-person narrator**. Unlike *Artemis Fowl*, this **narrator implies** the **skill** of the hero by showing us a **specific incident** which **illustrates** his **single-minded stealth** rather than simply stating his abilities.

- The other **key difference** between these stories is that *Reckless* uses a **conventional** story telling introduction 'Once upon a time ...' while *Artemis Fowl* **poses** a **direct question**.

- While *Artemis Fowl* **arouses** our **curiosity** by **employing hyperbole** to describe him as a 'child prodigy', the writer holds back any details for later in the story.

- *Reckless*, on the other hand, **immediately introduces** the **protagonist** in action, furtively entering his mother's room in **search** of information she refuses to give him.

- *Artemis Fowl* includes several examples of **alliteration** – '<u>t</u>est <u>t</u>hrown ' and '<u>v</u>illainous <u>v</u>enture', and one striking use of **onomatopoeia** in 'bamboozles'.

- *Reckless* is full of vivid **imagery**, effective use **of onomatopoeia** and **similes**.

A good approach to this **comparison** of two extracts should **include**:

- **Similarities** between the approaches adopted by the writers in **both stories** to **create character**.

- **Differences** between them in terms of **how** they **make** the central **characters come alive** on the page.

- Examples drawn from **both passages**.

- You should aim to make at least **three points** in your **comparison**, in each case **citing examples** and **explaining** the **effect** the words have on the reader.

- Show **how** the language helps to form the **fictional character** in your mind.

 L.O. R 7

Select key moments from texts and give thoughtful value judgements on:

- the main character
- a key scene
- a favourite image from a film, a poem, etc.

Unseen short story – narrator

Fictional prose texts include both longer stories called '**novels**' and shorter fiction called '**short stories**'. A **short story** is fiction that can be easily read in **one sitting**. Usually you will read a full short story in a single class period. During the three years leading up to your Junior Cycle exam, you will have read and studied many short stories and novels. For the purpose of your exam it is vital to revise and study *both* **short stories** and **novels**.

Short stories typically:

- Take place over a **short period of time** in a **single setting**.
- Involve a **small number** of well-drawn **characters**.
- Focus on the **build up** to and **consequences** of a single dramatic moment.

Sample questions and answers

Read the following opening paragraph from the short story 'The Ring' and read the questions and sample answer which follow.

The Ring

By Bryan MacMahon

I should like you to have known my grandmother. She was my mother's mother, and as I remember her she was a widow with a warm farm in the Kickham country in Tipperary. Her land was on the southern slope of a hill, and there it drank in the sun which, to me, seemed always to be balanced on the teeth of the Galtees. Each year I spent the greater part of my summer holidays at my grandmother's place. It was a great change for me to leave our home in a bitter sea-coast village in Kerry and visit my grandmother's. Why, man, the grass gone to waste on a hundred yards on the roadside in Tipperary was as much as you'd find in a dozen of our sea-poisoned fields. I always thought it a pity to see all that fine grass go to waste by the verge of the road. I think so still.

Question 1

Tick the appropriate box for each of the following statements.

1. A sunny 'farm' in 'Tipperary' is the ...

   a) plot

   b) setting   ✓

   c) scene

   ... for this story.

2. The **voice** of the **narrator** in the passage above is in the:

   a) first person ✓

   b) second person

   c) third person

3. The **phrase** 'the teeth of the Galtees' is an example of:

   a) alliteration

   b) onomatopoeia

   c) personification ✓

key point

Setting refers to the **unique time** and **place** in which a story happens. Settings can **create atmosphere**.

Question 2   *15 marks*

10

The **first-person narrator** draws us into the story with a style that is **intimate** and **confiding**. **Explain how** the writer achieves this **effect**.

Allow 10 minutes for 15-mark questions.

Sample answer

First of all, the **opening sentence** sounds like a friend expressing regret. 'I should like you to have known my grandmother.' It is like one person telling a **personal story** to someone they know and **trust**. This is a clever way to **entice** the readers to **trust the narrator** and his story.

Secondly, the speaker uses **colloquial phrases** like, '**Why man**, the grass ...' and 'a **bitter** sea-coast village'. This is an **informal conversational** style we use when we are on familiar terms with people. We imagine a narrator who is **casual**, speaking in a **relaxed** and **friendly tone**.

 **L.O. W 10**

Use and apply knowledge of language structures, for example

The third aspect of the style that is **intimate** is the **detail** of his **childhood visits**. His widowed grandmother lived on a 'warm farm' in the 'Kickham country' of 'Tipperary'. The farm had a **sunny aspect** on the 'southern slope of a hill'. This **attractive setting** is introduced by the narrator by means of a **flattering contrast** with the 'sea-poisoned' fields of his own home-place.

* sentence structure
* paragraphing
* grammar

to make writing a richer experience.

Studied fiction – prescribed novels and short stories

Your skills for **reading** and **analysing** fiction can be tested in both **unseen fiction** questions and questions about your **studied texts**. The Junior Cycle English specification requires you to study at least **two novels** from the **prescribed list** in Second and Third Year, as well as a **number** of **short stories**.

The **final part** of a fiction question might focus on the **novel** and/or **short stories** you have prepared in class with your teacher.

Challenge	The protagonist faces a difficult problem.
Conflict	A main character struggles against an opponent.
Climax	A high point of tension is reached.
Narrator	The storyteller in a novel or short story.
Plot	The pattern or key events in a story.
Resolution	The key question of the story reaches a conclusion.
Set up	Character and setting are introduced and described.
Themes	Main subjects, topics or issues explored in a story.

Plot, character, themes, narrator and the particular **writing style** of the author are the key areas to revise. Your answer should clearly **identify** the **title** of the **novel** or **story** and its **author**. Use correct punctuation by placing inverted commas around the title and capitalising the first letter in the key words, e.g. 'Wonder'; 'Of Mice and Men'; 'To Kill a Mockingbird'; 'His First Flight'; 'The Sniper'.

Marks are awarded for **accurate focus** on the question asked, backed up with **precise detail** from the story. It is good but not essential to **quote** from the text – often a specific reference is sufficient for full marks.

L.O. **W 3**

Write for a variety of purposes, for example to:
- analyse
- evaluate
- imagine
- explore, etc.

Revise your **novels** and **short stories** by **reading** and **making notes** on a number of **key moments**. Choose your **key moments** by selecting from the **five essential parts** of a narrative or **story arc**.

The graph below displays the classic arc or shape of a good story. The **level** of **excitement** or **tension** gradually **increases** from the **set up** to the **climax**. Key moments taken from the plot of 'Trash' by Andy Mulligan are used to illustrate how tension builds and falls.

Plot
A) Finding a bag
B) Police interrogation
C) Chased through town
D) Releasing the money
E) A new life for the boys

Excitement level

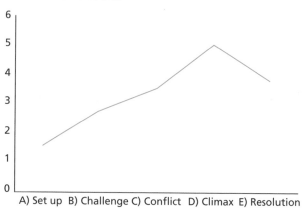

A) Set up B) Challenge C) Conflict D) Climax E) Resolution

Sample question and answer – key moment set-up

Of Mice and Men

By John Steinbeck

From a **novel** or **short story** you have studied, choose a character who experiences change.

> Revise **both** studied **novels** and at least **one short story**.

(a) **Describe** this **character** at the **beginning** of the novel or short story. *30 marks*

(b) **How** has the **character changed** by the **end** of the **novel** or **short story**? Support your answer by reference to the text. *30 marks*

Allow 20 minutes for 30-mark questions.

Sample answer (a)

(a) At the beginning of the novel *Of Mice and Men* by John Steinbeck, we meet the **hero** George. He is **described** as being 'small and quick, dark of face, with restless eyes and sharp, strong features'. We realise that George is mentally the more **alert** of the two characters as his friend Lennie is almost like a child in his innocence and simplicity. George assumes **authority** as he orders 'Lennie, for God's sakes don't drink so much.' **This is how we learn that George is in charge and for the duration of the story this remains the case**.

We also find out that although George has assumed responsibility for Lennie, he is growing **tired** of the trouble they get into together. He tells him he could 'get along so easy and so nice' if he didn't have to take care of Lennie.

The most attractive side of his personality is his **ability** to weave a dreamlike spell over an audience by **telling a story**. Lennie begs him to 'Tell how it's gonna be'. George then describes a utopian farm, a fantasy home for the pair of them. He paints a very attractive picture of a house where the two men could 'build up a fire in the stove and set around it an' listen to the rain comin' down on the roof'. This is their **dream**, a place of their own where they will not be bothered by anyone, but instead enjoy simple comfort and security.

On the other hand, George is also **realistic** and in anticipation of further trouble tells Lennie to meet him at this spot if anything bad happens. This shows his **ability** to **plan** a **strategy** in order to avoid **danger** in the future.

EXAMINER'S COMMENT

- **Clear focus** on physical **description** of the **hero** George.
- **Hero's character** is **explained** with **evidence** in the form of **quotations** from the **novel**.
- Answer is **fluently written** in clear prose and **well developed** over **five paragraphs**.
- **Additional points** deal with George's **storytelling ability** and his awareness of the **need** to have a **plan** to deal with any **future trouble**.

MARKS AWARDED: **Ex. 30/30** (90–100%) Distinction

Sample answer (b)

(b) At the end of the novel George is **still the wiser** of the two men. He is still well able to tell a story as he uses the fantasy of their little farm with the rabbits to distract George while he shoots him. His plan to meet at this spot should any trouble arise proves to be helpful as George has accidentally killed Curley's wife and had to flee for his life.

The crucial **difference** in George is that he now realises there is no hope for Lennie. In the beginning he thought they could overcome the problems they had in 'Weed' by running away to work in a different part of the country. Now he knows there is no point in running. This time Lennie has broken the law in a fatal way. By killing Curley's wife, he has endangered his own life. He will be killed either by Curley and Carlson, or later by execution for the crime of murder. **George appreciates** how **serious** this is, but **Lennie cannot fully understand** his **predicament**. For this reason, George reluctantly decides to kill his good friend.

George has changed in another key way. He now has had to **forsake his idyllic dream world**. The farm where he and Lennie and possibly old Candy would live in harmony feeding Lennie's rabbits and living off the 'fatta da lan' will never come to pass. George's dream is not going to happen and instead of a future of peace he must face the awful prospect of Lennie being cruelly killed for the crime of murder.

Previously when bad things happened George would give out to Lennie. At the end of the story when they meet in the woods beside the Salinas river Lennie asks him 'Ain't you gonna give me hell?' This time there is no need for George to scold Lennie. George has **changed in his attitude towards his friend**; it is pointless to try to teach him how to behave in the future.

EXAMINER'S COMMENT

- A **clear comparison** is made between the **character** of George in the **opening scene** and his attitudes and behaviour at the **end** of the novel.
- Answer **refers back** to points made in part (a) **outlining similarities** and **differences** in the **hero**.
- **Contrast** is **supported** by well-chosen **quotation** and **specific reference** to **plot points**.
- **Structure** and **expression fluent** throughout the answer.

MARKS AWARDED: Ex. 30/30 (90–100%) Distinction

Studied novel – dialogue

In revising both of your **studied novels** and a number of **short stories**, you must pay close attention to key **features** of the **writer's style**. You can make **notes** as you read again your five **key moments** from the stories. A **key moment** may be a **short paragraph** or it could extend over **several pages**.

key point

Conflict is **tension** in a situation. The **resolution** is the **final outcome** of that **conflict**.

A key moment in the novel *True Grit* by Charles Portis is the **courtroom drama** where Mattie Ross learns a great deal about Marshall Ruben 'Rooster' Cogburn and confirms her **decision** to hire him to pursue Tom Chaney, the outlaw who murdered her father.

In this scene, Rooster is giving evidence in the trial of Odus Wharton. *Mean Business* is the title of a graphic novel treatment of *True Grit*. The illustration on the following page of the courtroom scene highlights the **tension** between the characters.

> **L.O. R 1**
>
> Read texts with fluency, understanding and competence, decoding groups of words/ phrases and not just single words.

MR. BARLOW: What happened to Marshal Potter? *Dramatic formatting of characters' names*

MR. COGBURN: He died in this city six days later of septic fever. Leaves a wife and six babies.

MR. GOUDY: An objection. *Legal jargon adds realism*

JUDGE PARKER: Strike the comment.

MR. BARLOW: What became of Odus Wharton?

MR. COGBURN: There he sets.

MR. BARLOW: You may ask, Mr. Goudy.

MR. GOUDY: Thank you, Mr. Barlow. How long did you say you have been a deputy marshal, Mr. Cogburn?

MR. COGBURN: Going on four years. *Colloquial language establishes character*

MR. GOUDY: How many men have you shot in that time?

MR. COGBURN: I never shot nobody I didn't have to.

MR. GOUDY: That was not the question. How many? *Witness is being evasive. Hiding guilt?*

MR. COGBURN: Shot or killed? **MR. GOUDY:** Let us restrict it to 'killed' so that we may have a manageable figure. How many people have you killed since you became a marshal for this court?

> **L.O. W 8**
>
> Write about the effectiveness of key moments from texts, commenting on
> - characters
> - key scenes
> - favourite images
>
> from a film, a poem, a drama, a chapter, a media or web-based event.

MR. COGBURN: Around twelve or fifteen, stopping men in flight and defending myself.

MR. GOUDY: Around twelve or fifteen. So many that you cannot keep a precise count. Remember that you are under oath. I have examined the records and a more accurate figure is readily available. Come now, how many?

MR. COGBURN: I believe them two Whartons made twenty-three.

Violent character/formal register

MR. GOUDY: I felt sure it would come to you with a little effort. Now let us see. Twenty-three dead men in four years. That comes to about six men a year.

MR. COGBURN: It is dangerous work.

MR. GOUDY: So it would seem. And yet how much more dangerous for those luckless individuals who find themselves being arrested by you.

Sample questions and hints – studied fiction

b) From a novel or short story that you studied, show how the author's choice of words helped to build an interesting scene.　　**25 marks**

b) Outline your own personal response to that key scene from your chosen story.　　**25 marks**

Hints

- Use your notes to show **how** the writer builds a **key moment**. Writers use language to create a world for the story. For example in the extract above, the author uses **dialogue** to show **contrasting attitudes** between **two characters**. The **witness** uses **colloquial language** and is **evasive** with his answers. The **legal professionals**, on the other hand, use a more **formal register** appropriate to the **serious** nature of their **work**.

 L.O. R 8

Read texts to understand and appreciate language enrichment by examining
- an author's choice of words
- the use and effect of simple figurative language
- vocabulary and language patterns
- images

as appropriate to the text.

- Discuss the **formal** way the author **arranges** the **text** on the page. For instance in *True Grit*, the writer chose to format the scene with the **speaker's names** in bold print along the **left-hand margin** of the page. The scene looks like a **script** or **screenplay** for a play or film. This way of laying out the text on the page emphasises the **dramatic** nature of the scene.

- Most key moments will include some lines of **dialogue**. Dialogue communicates **emotion**. The tension in the scene is heightened as the question and answer style of **interrogation** creates **excitement**. The witness, Rooster, is **defensive** in his answers, while his opponent Goudy expresses his **disbelief** and **irritation** with partial answers.

- Learn **quotes** from your key moments to help illustrate the points you wish to make about the writer's **style**.

Studied short story

You will need to **make notes** about your **short stories** as you revise for the Junior Cycle exam. As you read a short story, use a **checklist** like the example below to keep a **record** of important **details** you may need to refer to in answering questions on the story. The examples used here are from 'The Sniper' by Liam O'Flaherty. **Choose** a **favourite** short story and use the grid and headings to make notes for your own revision.

Title	'The Sniper'
Author	Liam O'Flaherty
Characters – hero	• Republican sniper hiding on a rooftop • Ruthless – eyes 'cold gleam of the fanatic' • Efficient killer – 'woman whirled round and fell with a shriek' • Injured – 'A paroxysm of pain swept through him' • Young & clever student • Ingenious plan – 'dropped his left hand ... and let it hang, lifelessly' • Regret – 'lust of battle died in him' 'bitten by remorse'
Characters – villains	• His Free State Army enemies, 'armoured car' 'grey monster' • Opposing sniper – 'a good shot, whoever he was' • old woman informer 'pointing to the roof' where he lay
Setting	• Dublin city central 'dark waters of the Liffey' – image • 'O'Connell Bridge', 'Four Courts' • 1922 Irish Civil War bullets 'flash '& 'whizzed' • Guns – 'like dogs barking on lone farms' = simile
Themes	• Political violence and sudden death • Tragic loss of family • Excitement and horror of warfare
Key moments – Opening scene	• 'beleaguered Four Courts' • 'heavy guns roared' • hungry young sniper • cigarette gives him away
Climax	• Victorious, 'cry of joy' • Enemy soldier 'crumpled and fell forward'

Resolution/ending	• *Twist in the tale/tail* • *Enemy's identity revealed* • *Sniper 'looked into his brother's face'*
Personal response:	• *Enjoyed the tension and drama of guerrilla warfare* • *I admired the young hero's bravery and clever tactics* • *Sympathised with his horror at the end of the story* • *Wonder about how his enemy was thinking/feeling*
Lessons you learned	• *Horror and intensity of warfare* • *Success is often short lived and bittersweet*

If you have learned and **highlighted** significant **quotations**, you should try to include them as **support** in your answer. Otherwise, full marks can still be attained by means of an answer that makes **specific reference** to **key scenes** from the story.

Remember: The most important point is to **answer the question** you are asked. For each point you make, give a specific piece of evidence from the text and clarify what you mean by developing your idea into a short paragraph.

Where options are given, **never attempt extra questions** in your exam. You will run out of time.

Exam Question 2017 (SEC Junior Cycle Paper 3)

Section B – Responding to Studied Texts – Places I Encountered in my Reading

In the boxes provided below, give the titles and authors of two of the novels you have studied on your course. Marks are awarded for giving full titles and names with correct spelling.

First Novel	Second Novel
Title:	Title:
Author:	Author:

Question 1   *25 marks*

Compare the settings of your two chosen novels using the three following headings to guide your response: Physical Location; Mood or Atmosphere; Social Values.

Choose one important character from each of the two novels you have selected.

Name of character from first novel:	Name of character from second novel:

_____

_____

_____

_____

_____

_____

_____

_____

_____

_____

Question 2   *25 marks*

Which one of your chosen characters was more influenced by the world that he or she lived in? Explain your answer giving examples. Refer to both of your chosen characters in your answer.

_____

_____

_____

_____

_____

_____

_____

_____

_____

_____

_____

7 Studied Poetry

In the course of your three years as a **Junior Cycle** student you have read many **poems**. Questions on **Studied Poetry** will test your **understanding** of the **poems** you have **explored in class**. To be well prepared, you must **select a group** of up to **ten poems** in order to be able to answer the range of possible questions in this section. The poems you choose should be selected based on your answers to the following questions.

1. **Identify** the poem you like the **best** and the **name** of the poet who wrote it:

   Title: _The lake_

   Poet: _Roger McGough._

   Identify the poem you like the **least** and the **name** of the poet who wrote it:

   Title: _Everyone Song_

   Poet: _Siegfried Sassoon_

   Explain by **comparing** the two, **why** you liked one and disliked the other.

   ➡ **L.O. R 2**

   Read for a variety of purposes:
   - learning
   - pleasure
   - research
   - comparison

2. Name **two poems**, written **by different people**, dealing with a **similar theme**. The key is to select two poems where different poets have explored a **similar idea** or topic, but each dealt with it in a **distinct way**. Use a **grid** like the example given below.

Poem	Poet	Theme
'I Wandered Lonely as a Cloud'	William Wordsworth	Nature and memory
'Miracle On St David's Day'	Gillian Clarke	Nature, poetry and memory

3. **Identify** a **poet** whose work you **enjoyed** and give the **titles** of two poems you studied by that poet. This is sometimes called a **'case study'**. Over the course of your Junior Cycle you will have encountered **several poets** more than once. **Choose** one you **liked**. Pick **two memorable poems** by that poet and think about **why** you enjoyed reading them.

Gillian Clarke   Maya Angelou   Seamus Heaney   Siegfried Sassoon

4. Select **two poems** you studied which contain **curious** or **interesting images**. Very often you will remember a poem because of the **striking pictures** the poem **creates** in your mind. These images will include **detail** and usually **arouse intense emotion,** perhaps positive or negative feelings, or both. Make your selection and **learn the lines** which capture the most **powerful images**. Pay close attention as these **images** may be straightforward **descriptions** or involve more **figurative** language such as **similes** and **metaphors**.

5. Find **two poems** where the poet made **clever use** of the **sound** of words in the poem. Poetry began as an **oral** medium long before people had the skills to read and write words. **Rhyme, rhythm, onomatopoeia, alliteration** and **assonance** are just some of the ways the **sound** made by a **word**, or even a **letter**, can be significant in a poem.

6. Choose **two poems** which **arouse intense feelings** in you.

In choosing poems you should find that some poems will satisfy more than one of the **criteria** above. A **good selection** of poems will include enough to cover the **range** of possible questions outlined above.

You should know the **title** of the poem, the **name** of the **poet** and a number of **useful quotations**. The poetry question will require you to **discuss** the poem carefully and **focus** your answer on the questions asked of you. It is vital to support your answer with **precise** and **accurate** **quotations** from the poem. Some of your poems will be short and easier to learn because of the poet's use of **rhyme**, **rhythm** and other sound effects. A wise selection will take these factors into consideration.

Above all, you must give some thought to **your reasons** for choosing certain poems. Many poetry questions have required students to give their own **individual personal response** to a **favourite** poem or to show how a poem helped you to **make sense** of some area of **your own life**. For this reason, you must be able to say **why** you have chosen certain poems.

It is also important to know the **meaning** of some of the words used when discussing poetry. A sample list of studied poems and the reasons for choosing them is given below.

L.O. W 3

Write for a variety of purposes, for example to:

- analyse
- evaluate
- imagine
- explore, etc.

Revise your studied poetry by:

- Selecting up to **ten poems**.
- **Learning** key **quotations**.
- Making clear **notes** on the **themes** and **style** of each poem.

- **Case study poet: Seamus Heaney**
  1. 'Mid-Term Break'   Seamus Heaney
  2. 'Digging'   Seamus Heaney
- **Sound effects**
  3. 'Base Details'   Siegfried Sassoon
  4. 'Phenomenal Woman'   Maya Angelou
- **Imagery**
  5. 'The Lake Isle of Innisfree'   W.B. Yeats
  6. 'Stopping by Woods on a Snowy Evening'   Robert Frost
- **Theme comparison**
  7. 'I Wandered Lonely as a Cloud'   William Wordsworth
  8. 'Miracle On St David's Day'   Gillian Clarke
- **Personal response**
  9. 'Mid-Term Break'   Seamus Heaney
  10. 'The Lake Isle of Innisfree'   W.B. Yeats

1. Case study poet

Think carefully before you **choose** a 'case study' poet. The poet whose work you know **best** will be the writer you know well because you have **read**, **discussed** and **analysed more than one poem** by that poet. **Two substantial poems** may be sufficient. Revising these poems should include writing the poems out neatly and **comparing** them to identify **common features** of the poet's work. These **typical aspects** can be broken down into three separate but linked areas: **themes**, **style** and **personal response**.

L.O. R 8

Read texts to understand and appreciate language enrichment by examining

- an author's choice of words
- the use and effect of simple figurative language
- vocabulary and language patterns
- images

as appropriate to the text.

Themes are the writer's **preoccupations** – topics to which he or she keeps returning in their poems. **Style** refers to the distinctive **way** that person **uses language** in their poetry.

Personal response is your own **individual response** to the poem. It includes your **initial reaction** as well as **later reflection** on the **thoughts** and **feelings** brought up by the poem. A simple way to pick out the relevant quotations is to **highlight** them in a **colour-coded pattern** and **make notes** in the margin of the page to clarify the points you have noticed. The worked example below deals with two very popular poems by Ireland's recent Nobel Prize-winning poet, the late Seamus Heaney.

Mid-Term Break
By Seamus Heaney

I sat all morning in the college sick bay
Counting bells knelling classes to a close.
At two o'clock our neighbours drove me home.

In the porch I met my father crying—
He had always taken funerals in his stride—
And Big Jim Evans saying it was a hard blow.

The baby cooed and laughed and rocked the pram
When I came in, and I was embarrassed
By old men standing up to shake my hand

And tell me they were 'sorry for my trouble'.
Whispers informed strangers I was the eldest,
Away at school, as my mother held my hand

In hers and coughed out angry tearless sighs.
At ten o'clock the ambulance arrived
With the corpse, stanched and bandaged by the nurses.

Next morning I went up into the room. Snowdrops
And candles soothed the bedside; I saw him
For the first time in six weeks. Paler now,

Wearing a poppy bruise on his left temple,
He lay in the four-foot box as in his cot.
No gaudy scars, the bumper knocked him clear.

A four-foot box, a foot for every year.

Onomatopoeia   *Striking Imagery*   *Colloquial language*   *Alliteration*   *Emotive ending*

Digging
By Seamus Heaney

Between my finger and my thumb
The squat pen rests: snug as a gun.

Under my window, a clean rasping sound
When the spade sinks into gravelly ground:
My father, digging. I look down

Till his straining rump among the flowerbeds
Bends low, comes up twenty years away
Stooping in rhythm through potato drills
Where he was digging.

The coarse boot nestled on the lug, the shaft against the
  inside knee was levered firmly.
He rooted out tall tops, buried the bright edge deep
To scatter new potatoes that we picked
Loving their cool hardness in our hands.

By God, the old man could handle a spade.
Just like his old man.

My grandfather could cut more turf in a day
Than any other man on Toner's bog.
Once I carried him milk in a bottle
Corked sloppily with paper. He straightened up
To drink it, then fell to right away
Nicking and slicing neatly, heaving sods
Over his shoulder, digging down and down
For the good turf. Digging.

The cold smell of potato mould, the squelch and slap
Of soggy peat, the curt cuts of an edge
Through living roots awaken in my head.
But I've no spade to follow men like them.

Between my finger and my thumb
The squat pen rests.
I'll dig with it.

Onomatopoeia   *Striking Imagery*   *Colloquial language*   *Alliteration*   *Emotive ending*

Themes: Both 'Mid-Term Break' and 'Digging' deal with **intense memories** from the poet's **childhood**. Events that shaped him in positive and negative ways are explored here with details from his **early life** in **rural Ireland**. Each poem **concludes** with a strong line expressing **intense emotion** and indicating how the key moments outlined made a strong impact on the writer.

Style: Sound is a **vital element** in both poems. Heaney uses **onomatopoeia** to bring us directly into the heart of the scenes by recreating sounds, for example how the baby **'cooed'** while the neighbours **'whispered'**, and the noise his father's spade makes is **'rasping'**.

Alliteration also appears in both poems and the effect it has is to operate like a type of echo. The 'f' sound in the last three lines of 'Mid-Term Break' highlights the **grim finality of the child's death**. In 'Digging', the repeated 'd' sounds help to capture the repeated noise of the action of **going deep into the earth** with a spade.

Colloquial language: Irish phrases are used in both poems to give authentic and realistic detail of recognisable language we use in offering condolences (**'sorry for my trouble'**) or referring to his father as **'the old man'**.

Imagery: Heaney creates **memorable pictures** in our minds with the image of the child's **'corpse stanched and bandaged'** but also with the metaphor of the **'poppy bruise on his left temple'**. In a similar way, he returns to the **unusual simile** of the pen he is using to write his poem resting **'snug as a gun'** in his hand in 'Digging' as a way of letting us know that he will continue the family tradition of digging but in a **metaphorical** way rather than in the literal style of his ancestors.

These **notes** will be helpful in answering any Junior Cycle exam question where you are asked to discuss typical features of a poet's work and the **impact** that poetry has on you as a reader. Remember to also make notes on the **effect** the poems have on you as you read them – both your **thoughts** and your **feelings**.

2. Sound in poetry

In the notes on Heaney's poetry on the previous page, reference is made to **alliteration** and **onomatopoeia**, two typical ways he uses **sound** to **communicate** to us in his poetry. The examples below **develop** this key area by **identifying** and **explaining** several **additional important sound effects** in two very different poems by a pair of popular poets. By studying the examples below you will learn how to make notes on two poems where **sound** is a crucial feature of the writer's **style**. While 'Base Details' makes strong use of the **alliteration** and **onomatopoeia** discussed earlier, it is also important to highlight the impact of **assonance and end rhyme** in this poem. The **repetition** of **broad vowel sounds** in 'Majors ... base', 'Guzzling and gulping' and 'last scrap' **emphasises harsh sounds** and underlines the **angry tone** of this political **satire**.

> **L.O. R 13**
>
> Appreciate a variety of registers and understand their use in the written context.

Base Details		**Phenomenal Woman**	
By Siegfried Sassoon		By Maya Angelou	
If I were fierce, and bald, and short of breath,	A	Pretty women wonder where my secret lies.	A
I'd live with scarlet Majors at the Base,	B	I'm not cute or built to suit a fashion model's size	A
And speed glum heroes up the line to death.	A	But when I start to tell them,	
You'd see me with my puffy petulant face,	B	They think I'm telling lies.	A
Guzzling and gulping in the best hotel,	C	I say,	
Reading the Roll of Honour. 'Poor young chap,'	D	It's in the reach of my arms,	
I'd say – 'I used to know his father well;	C	The span of my hips,	B
Yes, we've lost heavily in this last scrap.'	D	The stride of my step,	
And when the war is done and youth stone dead,	E	The curl of my lips.	B
I'd toddle safely home and die – in bed.	E	I'm a woman	C

Assonance   Rhyme   Anaphora

Phenomenally.   D
Phenomenal woman,   C
That's me.   D

I walk into a room
Just as cool as you please,   E
And to a man,
The fellows stand or
Fall down on their knees.   E
Then they swarm around me,
A hive of honey bees.   E
I say,
It's the fire in my eyes,
And the flash of my teeth,
The swing in my waist,
And the joy in my feet.
I'm a woman
Phenomenally.

Phenomenal woman,
That's me.

The sun of my smile,
The ride of my breasts,
The grace of my style.

Assonance   *Rhyme*   *Anaphora*

Anaphora is a type of **repetition** which is, in effect, a type of rhyme. When a word, or words, are **repeated at the beginning of successive phrases** or **lines**, it creates an intensity that we usually find in persuasive speeches. Maya Angelou uses it to give **rhythm** to her poem 'Phenomenal Woman'. The impact of the repetition operates like a **heartbeat** running throughout the poem, e.g.:

> '*the fire in my* eyes,
> And *the flash of my* teeth,
> *The swing of my* waist,
> And *the joy in my* feet.'

This **driving rhythm** is a perfect way to underline the **energetic confidence** expressed in the poem.

Finally, a key difference between the **patterns** of **sound** in '**Base Details**' and '**Phenomenal Woman**' is the absence of any **refrain** or **chorus** in Sassoon's poem and the central importance of the repeated lines in Angelou's poem. The key lines in question are:

> *'I'm a woman*
> *Phenomenally.*
> *Phenomenal woman,*
> *That's me.'*

Watch the video 'This Girl Can: Phenomenal Woman' on YouTube

This **refrain** repeated at the end of each section of the poem operates as a **rhythmic slogan** and captures the essence of the poet's key idea; all aspects of women are 'phenomenal' and must be celebrated with pride. Even though both poems make use of many techniques to produce effective sounds, it is the **rhyme, rhythm** and **chorus** in 'Phenomenal Woman' that make it ideal for singing or rapping.

You can observe this **musical quality** in the video 'This Girl Can: Phenomenal Woman' on YouTube. The poem is spoken by the poet and set to music which perfectly illustrates the **sounds** of the poem and their **effectiveness**.

L.O. W 7

Respond imaginatively in writing to texts, showing a critical appreciation of:
- language
- style and content
- choice of words
- language patterns
- tone
- images

3. Powerful imagery

The best poets use **words** to put **pictures** in our **heads** that remain with us because they **evoke strong feelings**. When you are putting together your **list of studied poems**, it is vital to select at least **two poems** where the **images** have made a **lasting impact** on you.

- **Think** about the poems that have **stayed** with you **long after** you first read them.
- Ask yourself which **lines** from those poems **create powerful graphic images** in your mind.
- Next, **highlight** and **learn the lines** and make **notes** on precisely **how** each phrase made a **strong impression** on your **imagination**.

Two popular examples often studied for Junior Cycle poetry are 'The Lake Isle of Innisfree' by W. B. Yeats and 'Stopping by Woods on a Snowy Evening' by Robert Frost.

The Lake Isle of Innisfree
By W.B. Yeats

I will arise and go now, and go to Innisfree,
And a small cabin build there, of clay and wattles made:
Nine bean-rows will I have there, a hive for the honey-bee;
And live alone in the bee-loud glade.

And I shall have some peace there, for peace comes dropping slow,
Dropping from the veils of the morning to where the cricket sings;
There midnight's all a glimmer, and noon a purple glow,
And evening full of the linnet's wings.

I will arise and go now, for always night and day
I hear lake water lapping with low sounds by the shore;
While I stand on the roadway, or on the pavements grey,
I hear it in the deep heart's core.

Stopping by Woods on a Snowy Evening
By Robert Frost

Whose woods these are I think I know.
His house is in the village though;
He will not see me stopping here
To watch his woods fill up with snow.

My little horse must think it queer
To stop without a farmhouse near
Between the woods and frozen lake
The darkest evening of the year.

He gives his harness bells a shake
To ask if there is some mistake.
The only other sound's the sweep
Of easy wind and downy flake.
The woods are lovely, dark and deep,
But I have promises to keep,
And miles to go before I sleep,
And miles to go before I sleep.

Powerful imagery

Sample question and hints

Question 1

Choose a poem from the poems you studied for Junior Cycle English and identify strong images from the poem, explaining the impact the imagery had on you.

Always highlight key words in a question to keep your focus sharp.

Hints

Revising **imagery** is all about **highlighting, analysing** and **learning** the **key phrases** from a poem that made a **clear** and **powerful impression** on your **mind**. A good way to **record** this as you revise your studied poetry is to make a **simple grid** like the example below.

Poem	Image/evidence	Impact
'The Lake Isle of Innisfree' By W.B. Yeats	'small cabin build there, of clay and wattles'	Details of size and simple materials Adventure of a den or secret hiding place
	'midnight's all a glimmer, and noon a purple glow'	Colour and light make the place seem magically beautiful
	'lake water lapping with low sounds by the shore'	Peaceful picture of gentle waves at the lakeside
	'I stand on the roadway, or on the pavements grey'	Contrasting image of the dull concrete streets and buildings in the city
'Stopping by Woods on a Snowy Evening' By Robert Frost	'woods fill up with snow'	Gradual build-up of white snow against a background of tree trunks is an attractive mid-winter scene
	'Between the woods and frozen lake'	Location is remote, rural and very cold – hostile landscape
	'harness bells a shake'	Comical image of the horse showing his impatience by shaking his head
	'woods are lovely, dark and deep'	Picturesque forest scene holds the promise of beauty but also a hint of danger

You may like to **use the grid** on the previous page if you have **studied these two poems**. If not, then use the blank **template** below to **identify two poems** where the **images made a powerful impact** on you. Write out the **key phrases** for **four images** from each poem in the **second column**, and **your thoughts** and **feelings** about each image in the **final column**.

Poem	Image/evidence	Impact
Dulce Decorum est et Willfrid owen.	all went lare all blind Drunk with fortunge deaf even to the hoots of gas shells dropping behind.	surreal. real image at zombies.

4. Theme comparison

It is very important to think about how **two different poets** have dealt with the same **theme** or **topic**. Choose **two poems** with a **similar theme** and think about what makes the poems **like each other** and **how they differ**. A good way to organise your revision is to **list** the various **similarities** and **differences**. You can use the **key words** you have learned when analysing poetry as a form of **checklist**.

 L.O. W 7

Respond imaginatively in writing to texts, showing a critical appreciation of:

- language
- style and content
- choice of word
- language patterns
- tone
- images

Title 1	*After ne tinesic.*	Title 2	
Poet 1		Poet 2	
Theme		Theme	
Tone		Tone	
Imagery		Imagery	
Metaphor		Metaphor	
Characters		Characters	
Symbols		Symbols	
Sound		Sound	
Setting		Setting	

Sample question and answer

Question 2   30 marks

Identify two poems you have studied which deal with the same theme in different ways.

A. Name the poems and poets.   6 marks

B. Identify the theme common to both poems.   4 marks

 **20**

Allow 20 minutes for 30-mark questions.

Title: *After ne titonic*	Title: *Lake Isle of Innishree*
Poet: *Derecen Maren*	Poet: *WB Yeats*
Theme: *Memory .*	

C. Discuss **two ways** in which the poems are **like** each other in their **treatment** of the **key idea**.

Support the **points** you make with **suitable quotation** from the poems.

10 marks

Both poems refer to the character wanting to go back to a past time or place, wether to undo mistakes made in the case of after the titanic or simply because it is a peaceful and happy place in the case of Isle of Innisfree. Both poems treat the respective locations in a dream like fashion, exaggerating features of it, for example, the peacefulness of the isle [at night] is exagerated in the line 'the ~~means~~ [midnights] all a glimmer' in Isle of Innisfree.

D. **Explain one way** in which the poems are **different** in what they say on that **topic**.

Support the **points** you make with **suitable quotation** from the poems.

10 marks

Whereas Isle of innisfree is mostly positive and wishful, after the titanic is heavily regretful and almost depressing. Whereas yeats wants to return to the Island as it is a comforting place for him, the man in After the titanic wishes to return to the night the titanic sunk as he is deeply ashamed of what he did to escape, saying; I tell you I sank as far as any Hero'.

exam focus

- Learn the **full title** and **poet's name**.
- Answer the **full** question.
- Always put **titles in inverted commas** and use **capitals** for **main words** in titles and for both the **first name** and **surname** of the **poet**, e.g. 'Miracle On St David's Day' by Gillian Clarke.
- Write in **full sentences** and **paragraphs**.
- Give your own **personal response**, e.g. 'I like ...'.
- **Explain** your points (give reasons), e.g. '... because'.
- Give **evidence** in the form of **quotations**.

The poems below are linked as they both deal with the **same themes** or topics. They are also connected, as one poem, 'Miracle On St David's Day', is **influenced** or **inspired by** the earlier poem, 'I Wandered Lonely as a Cloud' (also referred to as 'The Daffodils').

I Wandered Lonely as a Cloud
By William Wordsworth

I wandered lonely as a cloud
That floats on high o'er vales and hills,
When all at once I saw a crowd,
A host, of golden daffodils;
Beside the lake, beneath the trees,
Fluttering and dancing in the breeze.

Continuous as the stars that shine
And twinkle on the milky way,
They stretched in never-ending line
Along the margin of a bay:
Ten thousand saw I at a glance,
Tossing their heads in sprightly dance.

The waves beside them danced; but they
Out-did the sparkling waves in glee:
A poet could not but be gay,
In such a jocund company:
I gazed – and gazed – but little thought
What wealth the show to me had brought:

For oft, when on my couch I lie
In vacant or in pensive mood,
They flash upon that inward eye
Which is the bliss of solitude;
And then my heart with pleasure fills,
And dances with the daffodils.

Miracle On St David's Day
By Gillian Clarke
*'They flash upon that inward eye
which is the bliss of solitude?'*
(from 'The Daffodils' by William Wordsworth)

An afternoon yellow and open-mouthed
with daffodils. The sun treads the path
among cedars and enormous oaks.
It might be a country house, guests strolling,
the rumps of gardeners between nursery shrubs.

I am reading poetry to the insane.
An old woman, interrupting, offers
as many buckets of coal as I need.
A beautiful chestnut-haired boy listens
entirely absorbed. A schizophrenic

on a good day, they tell me later.
In a cage of first March sun a woman
sits not listening, not feeling.
In her neat clothes the woman is absent.
A big, mild man is tenderly led

to his chair. He has never spoken.
His labourer's hands on his knees, he rocks
gently to the rhythms of the poems.
I read to their presences, absences,
to the big, dumb labouring man as he rocks.

He is suddenly standing, silently,
huge and mild, but I feel afraid. Like slow
movement of spring water or the first bird
of the year in the breaking darkness,
the labourer's voice recites 'The Daffodils'.

The nurses are frozen, alert; the patients
seem to listen. He is hoarse but word-perfect.
Outside the daffodils are still as wax,
a thousand, ten thousand, their syllables
unspoken, their creams and yellows still.

Forty years ago, in a Valleys school,
the class recited poetry by rote.
Since the dumbness of misery fell
he has remembered there was music
of speech and that once he had something to say.

When he's done, before the applause, we observe
the flowers' silence. A thrush sings
and the daffodils are flame.

The example below illustrates how a **revision grid** can bring **focused revision** together and help produce a useful **study aid**. Notes like this are a very **efficient** way of **summarising key points** to read on the night before your exam.

Similarities	
'I Wandered Lonely as a Cloud'	**'Miracle On St David's Day'**
Themes: The beauty of nature/the power of memory	**Themes:** The beauty of nature/the power of memory
Characters: A man remembers daffodils.	**Characters:** A man remembers daffodils.
Imagery & symbol: Daffodils represent hope.	**Imagery & symbol:** Daffodils represent hope.
Key event: Something makes a lasting impression on the imagination – flowers.	**Key event:** Something makes a lasting impression on the imagination – poetry.
Numbers: *'Ten thousand saw I at a glance'*	**Numbers:** *'a thousand, ten thousand'*
Setting: Springtime	**Setting:** Springtime
Drama: A 'show' in nature.	**Drama:** The show is a human performance – a man *'recites'.*

Differences	
'I Wandered Lonely as a Cloud'	**'Miracle On St David's Day'**
Mood: Happy ➔ happier	**Mood:** Sad ➔ happy
Inspired by: The experience of nature and memory	**Inspired by:** The experience, and another poem, *'I wandered ...'*
Setting: Countryside and home	**Setting:** Nursing home
Metaphor: The poet compares flowers to people – personification.	**Metaphor:** The poet compares flowers to fire.
Movement : Flowers are free, *'fluttering and dancing'* *'tossing their heads'* Lake water, *'sparkling waves'*	**Stillness:** Flowers are motionless, *'still as wax'* People, *'boy listens'*; *'woman sits'*; *'nurses are frozen'*
Sound: Regular rhyme scheme ABABCC; onomatopoeia – *'fluttering' 'flash'*	**Sound:** Unrhymed lines Onomatopoeia – *'rocks'*; *'hoarse'*
Crowd: Flowers imagined as *'a crowd, a host'*	**Crowd:** The crowd is the audience – patients and nurses.
Wellbeing: Healthy person enjoying physical and mental freedom	**Wellbeing:** Patients suffer in a variety of ways and all are taken care of in a home

exam Q

Sample answer   *30 marks*

Title: *'I Wandered Lonely as a Cloud'*	**Title:** *'Miracle On St David's Day'*
Poet: *William Wordsworth*	**Poet:** *Gillian Clarke*
Theme: *The power of memory*	

One **similarity** between what both poets write on the theme of the **power of memory** is the way a remembered experience can **evoke strong feelings**. We see this in 'I Wandered Lonely as a Cloud' when Wordsworth writes about how, in a moment of solitude, the memory of the daffodils 'flash upon that inward eye' of the imagination. Recalling this **image** his heart 'with pleasure fills'.

This is like the moment in Gillian Clarke's poem when the patient in a nursing home stands to recite the Wordsworth poem he had learnt 'by rote' as a child 'forty years ago in a Valleys school'. **Both poems show how remembering can produce strong feelings.** In Clarke's poem when the man stands she feels 'afraid' until he speaks and when he is finished she, the nurses and the patients respond with 'applause'. This **joyous response** is like the 'pleasure' in Wordsworth's poem.

Both poets also make use of the key **image** of the 'daffodils' as a **colourful sight** which makes a **lasting impression** on the memory of people. Wordsworth uses **personification** when he writes of the flowers 'fluttering and dancing' as if they were alive. They have become a **symbol** for him of beauty and happiness; remembering the sight of them, the poet responds and his 'heart with pleasure fills and dances with the daffodils'.

Gillian Clarke also uses **personification** when she writes of an 'afternoon yellow and open-mouthed with daffodils'. It is as if the day and the flowers are about to speak. The poet's own **memory** of the day includes details of the 'creams and yellows' of the petals. When the 'labouring man' stands to speak, the implication is that both hearing poetry spoken out loud and the 'thousand' or 'ten thousand' daffodils

L.O. R 9

Identify, appreciate and compare the ways in which different literary, digital and visual genres and sub-genres shape texts and shape the reader's experience of them.

outside have **combined to give him back his voice**. For one glorious moment he 'remembered there was music of speech and that once he had something to say'. Like Wordsworth, the **imagery** of the **flowers** in springtime lived on in his memory and emerged in an unexpected way.

One key **difference** is that we do not know how the 'labouring man' was feeling even though he speaks for the first time in years. On the other hand, we know exactly how Wordsworth felt, as remembering made him feel that his heart was dancing 'with the daffodils'. **Unlike Wordsworth**, the man remembering in the second poem is not **alone**. The pleasure in 'Miracle On St David's Day' is felt by the audience of poet, patients and nursing staff who listen transfixed while the man who had been 'dumb' recites Wordsworth's poem 'hoarse but word-perfect'. His **memory** is not a solitary joy but instead brings people together in a moment where the **pleasure** is **shared**.

EXAMINER'S COMMENT
Indicators of quality:

- **Clarity** of **focus** on the task **comparing** different treatments of the same theme.
- A well-**structured** and **developed** response using **appropriate language** to analyse poems.
- Candidate **demonstrates** an **original** and **fresh approach** using well-chosen **quotes** for **support**.

MARKS AWARDED: Ex. 30/28 (90–100%) Distinction

5. Personal response

Finally, you must choose **two poems** where you have **strong opinions** about the **themes** or **topics** explored. Ask yourself which poems have **stayed with you most**, have caused you to **ask questions** about your own experiences, or **resonated** with you by shedding a **new light** on an important topic.

Personal response is about both **thoughts** and **feelings**. A poem like 'Mid-Term Break' might strike a chord with you because of its exploration of **grief**; 'The Lake Isle of Innisfree' might remind you of a **special place** which you consider **beautiful** or peaceful; 'Miracle On St David's Day' may **provoke questions** about how we think about issues around **mental health**.

It should be possible to **complete** your selection of **studied poems** by choosing two from the group of eight already selected which made a **profound impact** on you. Once you have made a list of **key points** and **selected supporting** quotations, your revision of studied poetry is complete.

It is vital that you consider the **various ways** in which a poem made an **impact** on you. How did you **react** when you **first read** or heard it in class? In what way did your **thoughts** or **feelings change** when you looked at the poem later on? The power of poetry is that our **response** to the same piece of writing can **develop** and **change** as we **grow** and learn.

Exam Question 2017 (SEC Junior Cycle Sample 3)

Section D – Appreciating Language – Poetry – Inspired by Place

Question 1   *30 marks*

Choose any two poems you have studied that you feel give you a strong sense of the place that they are set in. Give the poets' names and the titles of their poems. Marks are awarded for giving full titles and names with correct spelling.

20

Allow 20 minutes for 30-mark questions.

Title Poem 1:	Title Poem 2:
Poet's name:	Poet's name:
Optional Rough Work	

In your view, which one of the poets was more successful in conveying a sense of place in his/her poem? Support your analysis with detailed reference to both of your nominated poems.

_____

_____

_____

_____

_____

_____

_____

_____

_____

_____

8 Classroom-Based Assessment 1 – Oral Communication

In this section you will revise **Junior Cycle English** with specific focus on **Classroom-Based Assessment 1** in a number of different ways:

- **Summarising** elements of Junior Cycle **Assessment**.
- **Examining** the details of **classroom-based assessments** (CBA).
- Exploring **features of quality** for assessment.
- **Learning** about **descriptors** for **oral CBA**.
- **Considering** the range of **format options** for **oral CBA**.
- **Reading** a **checklist** of preparation required.
- Completing the **reflection note**.
- **Viewing recommendations** on how to **perform** or **present** your oral component.

Assessment overview

Assessment in Junior Cycle English has **several elements**. Your work will be awarded results in **four** distinct ways. Two elements known as **classroom-based assessments** are completed in Second and Third Year and that work will be **evaluated** by the **teachers** in your school. The **remaining two** parts are written and corrected by an **examiner** after your final Junior Cycle exam in **June** of **Third Year**.

Junior Cycle English results are **reported** in **two ways**:

1. September after your Junior Cycle Exam using the following grading system:

   Grading of the State-Certified Examinations
   - Distinction (90–100%)
   - Higher merit (75–89%)
   - Merit (55–74%)
   - Achieved (40–54%)
   - Partially achieved (20–39%)

2. As one section of your **Junior Cycle Profile of Achievement**.

	Element	Timing	Value
1.	Oral – CBA 1	Final term Second Year	Descriptor JCPA
2.	Written collection of texts – CBA 2	Christmas/spring Third Year	Descriptor JCPA
3.	Written assessment task	Third Year	10% Junior Cycle Result
4.	Final exam	June of Third Year	90% Junior Cycle Result

Classroom-based assessments

During the course of Second and Third Year as part of your Junior Cycle English course you will complete two **classroom-based assessments**. The purpose of these activities is to give you **focused feedback** on your **oral** and **written work** in English.

Classroom-based assessment	Format	Student preparation	Completion by:
Oral communication	Individual or group communication or presentation	During a period of three weeks, with support and guidance by teacher	End of Second Year
The collection of the student's texts	Two texts chosen by the student from his/her portfolio of texts	Texts produced over time with support and guidance by teacher	End of term 1, Third Year

Features of quality and levels of achievement

For both CBAs you will be awarded a **descriptor** which indicates the **level of success** you have **reached** in your oral or written work. The various **descriptors** are explained below:

Exceptional: The student's communication is remarkable for its fluency and its control of material used. The communication is imaginatively shaped to a very clear purpose. The student's engagement with the audience/listener is compelling and sustained.

Above expectations: The student's communication is clear and convincing, and material has been very well chosen. Communication is fully shaped to its intended purpose. Engagement with the audience/listener is highly effective.

In line with expectations: Communication is clear and convincing for the most part, showing knowledge of the subject of the communication. Communication is shaped to a purpose. Engagement with the audience/listener is reasonably well sustained.

Yet to meet expectations: Communication is unconvincing, although some knowledge of the subject of the communication is shown. The purpose of the communication is often unclear. Engagement with the audience/listener is haphazard or poorly sustained.

The **level of achievement** for CBAs will be determined by your own teacher in consultation with his/her colleagues in your school. You will be informed about how well you have performed in the CBA when you are awarded your **Junior Cycle Profile of Achievement**. The **descriptors** for English will appear alongside other information about your **achievements** in school during the years of your Junior Cycle.

Oral communication options

You will work in Second Year on your Oral Communications CBA. During class time your teacher will advise your class on how to choose a topic, methods for gathering information through focused research, and the skills required for effective oral communication.

You will aim to **speak** for **three minutes** on a **topic of your choice** in **class time**. Some of the oral presentations will be **recorded**. The **style** or oral communication you produce will be based on **ONE** of the following four options:

1. Performance	The student may participate in a scripted or improvised performance, including drama, alone or with others.
2. Presentation	The student may speak with or without notes. A reading of a prepared script is allowable.
3. Interview	The student may respond to questions asked by the teacher and/or other students; the student may assume the role of interviewer as well as respondent in a dialogue setting.
4. Response to stimulus material	Stimulus material – visuals, written text, aural text, and so on – may be used by the teacher and/or student/s to promote, prompt or guide oral communication.

Preparation and research

 **L.O. W 1**

Reflection note

As part of your preparation for your **oral communication** assessment you will be asked to complete a **student reflection note** by your teacher. In this note you will **outline** the **work** you have done in preparation for your **performance, presentation** or **interview**.

Demonstrate understanding that there is a clear purpose for all writing activities and be able to:

- plan
- draft
- re-draft
- edit

as appropriate.

Areas for reflection might include:

- **Specific tasks** you undertook in **preparation** for your assessment.
- **Sources** of information or data used in your talk.
- Key **lessons** you learned in preparing for this talk.
- Any areas you think you could **improve** on.

Choosing your format

If you have already built up **experience of performing** through **speech and drama** classes or in your work on **stage productions**, then you might choose the first option of **performance**. For this you may choose to perform **alone** or as part of a **group**. Experienced performers have the advantage of practice in the skills of **communicating clearly** to an audience. If you have

key point

In **choosing** a **format** and **topic** for your **oral CBA**, you must make clever use of **what you know well** already and any **previous experience** of speaking aloud to a group of people.

participated in competitions like 'Poetry Aloud' or inter-schools debating, then you will be confident of your ability to **project your voice** and convey **understanding** and **emotion**.

1. Performance

One **advantage** of selecting the performance option is that you do not face the same challenges to compose a meaningful text or message of your own. A **strong performance** of a drama extract or speech can be **moving** for an **audience** if the speaker **interprets** the **author's words well**. The challenge is not to come up with a fresh and original formula or words, but to **interpret** someone else's words for an audience. It certainly requires work,

 **L.O. O 7**

Choose appropriate language, style and visual content for specific audiences and chosen purposes:

- persuading
- informing
- narrating
- describing a process

but the **skill of interpreting** and **performing** is not the same as the skill of writing your own original work. You are free to **perform alone** if you wish, or to **combine with your classmates** to give a **choral reading** or **group dramatic performance**. Make your decision in **consultation** with your **teacher**, or as part of a group with your classmates.

2. Presentation

Many students will choose to make a **short presentation** to the class on a **subject** or topic they know well. Sample topics include:

- An interesting **sportsperson, performer, writer, film director, hobby**, etc.
- An **organisation** with which you are **involved**.
- An investigation of a **text, writer** or **film**.
- An **activity**, **interest** or **pastime** in which you are **involved**, e.g. music, sport, fashion, reading, drama, film, etc.

This **style** of oral communication is an ideal opportunity for you to use your **knowledge** and **experience** well to help boost your assessment result. Speak about a **topic you know well**, which you have **strong opinions** and **feel passionately** about. Check it out with your teacher.

Once you have chosen the theme or topic, it is vital to do some **research** to gather **helpful facts** or **data** to include in your talk. Solid **information** lends authority to your thoughts and opinions, and communicates to your audience that you are **in command** of **your subject**.

This can also prove useful after your talk, when the teacher may conduct a **short question** and **answer** session.

3. Interview

This option will follow the **format** of **question** and **answer** traditionally used in all interviews. You can be assessed as **either interviewer** or **interviewee**. It is an ideal opportunity for two students to collaborate by coming up with a **series** of **interesting questions** on a topic where one student has above-average knowledge of the subject.

L.O. O 12

Demonstrate how register, including grammar, text structure and word choice, varies with context and purpose in spoken texts.

In the course of the interview it may be useful to **include a prop** or **picture** to act as a **prompt** for a line of questioning, or to allow the person being interviewed to explain the relevance of the prop.

4. Visual aids

Some students will use projected images or animated **presentations** like **PowerPoint** or **Prezi** as a visual aid for their presentation. A word of warning: make sure you check the text of the PowerPoint carefully for **spelling** and **grammar**. Also make sure that you **practise speaking** while the visual presentation is running. **Lines** of text should appear **one by one** instead of in a block of text. When it comes to slides used to accompany a talk, the old adage '**less is more**' applies. Concentrate on **speaking well** to your audience. The **visual aids** are meant to **complement** your talk, not distract your listeners and divert their attention away from you.

5. Response to stimulus material

You have the option of building your oral communication around visual, written or aural **stimulus material**. Your thoughts on **a favourite singer**, a **key scene** from a **film** you love or a **discussion** of a **funny commercial** might make a refreshing presentation for your student audience. You could use a prompt supplied by your teacher or

choose one you know you can talk about with **confidence**. As with presentation slides, you must make sure the stimulus material does not divert your audience's attention away from your **spoken words**. You are being assessed for your skills in **oral communication** – do not undermine your performance by including elements that might weaken the concentration of those listening to you.

Quality oral communication

Ten top tips for giving a presentation

1. Know your subject well

We speak **fluently** when we **know** what we're **talking about. Choose** your **topic carefully**, making sure it is well **focused** on your personal **knowledge** and **experience**. This will make you **calm** and give you a **feeling of confidence** in your speech.

2. Practise until you feel confident

When you have completed the text of your talk, practise by **speaking it out loud alone** at first, then with an audience of one or two **attentive people. Listen** to any **advice** you get about pronunciation or **diction. Meaning** must come across **clearly** to your audience. When you feel **confident** you can speak well. Use your **brief notes** as a **reference** if necessary.

3. Stand up straight

Posture is one way **we communicate confidence. Lift your head** so that your voice can be heard. If you need to **look down** to check notes, **pause briefly**. Speaking while you face the floor will cause your audience to miss some words. Let your **shoulders relax**. We often hold **tension** in our neck and shoulders, which can make it difficult to **breathe freely**.

4. Breathe and relax

Take a few **deep breaths** before you speak and **breathe naturally** once your talk or performance **begins. Breathing** properly helps to **keep us calm** and **relaxed**. Also you need to breathe in order to **project your voice** and be **heard** by everyone listening.

5. Speak clearly

Your audience must be able to hear you. **Avoid shouting**. Projecting your voice depends on having a **good posture** and **opening your mouth** to let the sound fill the room. Remember to fit the **tone** of your voice to the **feeling expressed** or evoked by your words. **Silence** or a **deliberate pause** can be highly effective, as it gives the audience a moment to **think** about what you have said.

6. Take your time

You must speak for a minimum of **three minutes**. There will be no penalty if you exceed this time. It is most important that you **manage the pace** of your speaking voice. Adrenaline can cause us to rush and might mean that the audience miss out on a key point. Do not be afraid that you will run out of time.

7. Think about what you are saying

If you **think** about what you are saying, you will **express your understanding** well. When you **perform** a **poem** or **speech** or give a **presentation**, you have an advantage over your audience because you have **already read the text** several times. It is your job to **articulate the ideas and feelings** in a meaningful way. **Tone** of voice helps to **express meaning**.

8. Make eye contact

You will hold the **attention** of your listeners when you **make eye contact**. This quality of attention feeds back to you by making you **feel confident** that your words are **being heard** and **understood**. Do not be afraid to **slowly sweep the room**, looking into the left and right corners. **Everyone** will feel that they are **being addressed** by you. If you choose to **pause for effect,** then make sure you **look up directly** at your audience.

L.O. O 12

Demonstrate how register, including grammar, text structure and word choice, varies with context and purpose in spoken texts.

9. Speak in your own voice

Your own voice is unique to you and deserves to be heard. As long as you **pronounce words** clearly, you can be proud of your **accent** and **intonation**. It is **distinctive** and an important tool in your set of oral communication skills.

10. Use appropriate gestures

Movement, posture and **physical gestures** should be **deliberate, planned** and **meaningful.** You can use your hands and arms to **reinforce a key point** using a **suitable gesture.** Constant movement, however, might distract your audience from listening to what you are saying and is a sign that you are nervous. A **limited number** of **significant gestures** is a way of **underlining key moments** in your talk, **drawing extra attention** from your listeners.

Finally, think of the work of your **classmates** as a **valuable resource.** You will help your colleagues by **listening attentively** to them, but you can also pick up useful ideas by paying close attention to **how they communicate** with their audience. **Adopt** or **adapt** any skill that fits in well with your own performance or presentation.

Practise speaking aloud as much as possible, especially with help from a trusted friend or adult.

 L.O. O 8

Listen actively in order to interpret meaning, compare, evaluate effectiveness of, and respond to drama, poetry, media broadcasts, digital media, noting key ideas, style, tone, content and overall impact in a systematic way.

9 Classroom-Based Assessment 2 – Written Assessment

In this section you will prepare for your second classroom-based assessment – CBA 2 – collection of work revising:

- Junior Cycle **assessment overview**.
- Details of **Classroom-Based Assessment 2 (written)**.
- Selecting **collection of texts**.
- **Genres** and **feedback**.
- **Drafting** and **editing**.
- Completing the **written reflection note**.
- **Descriptors** for **CBA 2**.
- **Written assessment task**.
- **Sample question** and **sample answer**.

Assessment overview

Assessment in Junior Cycle English has **several elements**. Your work will be awarded results in **four** distinct ways. Two elements known as **classroom-based assessments** are completed in Second and Third Year; that work will be **evaluated** by the **teachers** in your school. The **remaining two** parts are written and corrected by an **examiner** after your final Junior Cycle exam in **June** of **Third Year**.

Element	Timing	Value
1. Oral – CBA 1	Final term Second Year	Descriptor JCPA
2. Written collection of texts – CBA 2	Christmas/Spring of Third Year	Descriptor JCPA
3. Written assessment task	Third Year	10% Junior Cycle Result
4. Final exam	June of Third Year	90% Junior Cycle Result

This unit will focus on **preparation** and **completion** of your **written assessment** during the course of Third Year. This is made up of two parts:

1. **Collection of texts**
2. **Written assessment task**

Submitting written work

In Third Year you will complete your **classroom-based assessment (CBA)** by submitting written work. This **assessment** will take place **in school** under the guidance of your teacher, and comprises two parts:

1. Collection of work – from a **range** of **written work** undertaken during **Second** and **Third Year**, you select the **two** you feel best reflect your **highest quality of writing**. These **two final drafts** of your work are **evaluated** by **your teacher**. Your **level** of **achievement** is awarded by a panel of teachers from your **school**.

2. Written assignment – when you have submitted two pieces of written work, your class will complete a **written assignment**. After listening to a video or audio stimulus on the **subject of writing**, your class will discuss **specific aspects** of the **writing process**. It could range from talking about **what inspires you** to **how you felt about getting feedback** on your work. You will answer a number of questions and your assignment score will be included with your Junior Cycle exam to be corrected in the summer.

Collection of work

As you work on **various written tasks** in Second and Third Year, you will **collect final drafts** of your best pieces in your **collection of work**. Think of this as a **portfolio** or **selection** of your personal 'greatest hits' in **Junior Cycle English**.

> **key point**
>
> All CBAs take place during normal class time in school. They are evaluated by your teacher, and the result is reported in your Junior Cycle Profile of Achievement.

It might include **imaginative pieces** of:

- fiction
- poems
- dramatic dialogues
- remodelling of texts you have studied

It could also comprise more **practical or functional genres** like:

- diaries
- interviews
- reports
- reviews
- letters
- speeches
- emails
- blogs

Your collection might also include some **quality analytical pieces** where you respond to a poem, drama, story or film, explaining the impact the writing made on you and outlining the various elements that made it memorable.

In essence, the collection can include **any original piece** of work you take pride in which helps to give an **accurate impression** of **your developing skill** as a **young writer**.

Over the span of your Junior Cycle you will attempt writing tasks and benefit from **feedback** from your **classmates** as well as your **teacher**. You will be encouraged to take on board the supportive suggestions to **improve** the **quality** of your writing by **editing** and **re-drafting** your work.

When you are happy with a piece of work, place it in a **secure folder** in the care of your teacher. As you write **new work** you think highly of, you may **add** to the **collection**, or indeed **replace texts**. The **final collection** must comprise **at least four written texts** in **four** different writing **genres**. From these four you will **choose** the **two** you feel are most suitable for the **final assessment**.

Your teacher will read the work again to award you a **level** of **achievement descriptor** based on the quality of your writing.

Genres and feedback

Your writing will always be based on a **specific task**. Think of each piece as an original written text aimed at a **specific audience** and intended to communicate a **focused message** in a **suitable style**.

Your teachers and classmates will offer **feedback**

 L.O. W 6

Use editing skills continuously during the writing process to enhance meaning and impact:

- select vocabulary
- reorder words, phrases and clauses
- correct punctuation and spelling
- reorder paragraphs
- remodel, manage content

 key point

Your collection of work must include at least four different genres and you must select the best two for your teacher to evaluate.

 L.O. W 4

Write competently in a range of text forms, for example:

- letter
- report
- multi-modal text
- review
- blog

using appropriate vocabulary, tone and a variety of styles to achieve a chosen purpose for different audiences.

and identify **technical aspects** that **work well** or **require improvement**. These skills of **reviewing**, **drafting** and **editing** are essential writing skills to develop in Junior Cycle English. Advice for changes might include:

- Punctuation, paragraphing and spelling.
- Overall structure or organisation of ideas.
- Form or shape based on guidelines for the genre.

Comments might focus on the **quality** of your **content**:

- The ideas explored.
- The themes developed.
- The consistency of focus in your writing.
- The original, or fresh, perspective you bring to an issue.

Finally, attention could be drawn to the **language you use**:

- Sophisticated and appropriate choice of vocabulary.
- Effective and memorable imagery.
- Sustained register suitable to the task and audience for your work.

Drafting and editing

The skill of writing involves several **distinct phases**. Very few writers face a blank page and write a complete finished poem, story or article perfectly first time.

The **stages of writing** well usually involve:

Inspiration	Something that prompts you to write; a spark igniting an idea in your mind.
Planning	Thinking about how to begin, develop and conclude your written work.
First draft	Your initial attempt to express your thoughts and feelings on a topic in a specific style.
Feedback	You give your work to someone to read and they outline the strengths and any problems with the writing.
Second draft	Your second version builds on the success of the first draft, making improvements.

It is useful to **think about changes** you make to a piece of **written work**. Ask yourself a number of important questions:

- What **words or sentences** work well? Why?
- Are there any words or sentences I can **delete** or **change** to fit in better with the text?
- Are there **points** I need to **develop** or **expand**?
- Does the writing **focus** on the **task** I was set?
- Is the **language appropriate** for the **audience** and **genre**?
- Do the **paragraphs** or **stanzas** **flow**, fitting together well?

 **L.O. W 6**

Use editing skills continuously during the writing process to enhance meaning and impact:

- select vocabulary
- reorder words, phrases and clauses
- correct punctuation and spelling
- reorder paragraphs
- remodel, manage content

Making your selection

Your **final selection of two pieces** should include **work you are pleased with** that reflects your **strengths** as a **young writer**. Take on board the **response of classmates and teachers** to your work. Sometimes other people notice **quality writing** where we can only see flaws or problems. A good writer is **open** to hearing **focused feedback** and only makes any **necessary changes** when they are required to improve the quality. **Change** must be **deliberate** and done for a specific and **valid reason**. This could prove to be significant in your **written assessment task** or **reflection note**. These two parts of your assessment might give you an opportunity to reflect on what you learned about yourself as a writer by completing a particular task.

L.O. W 11

Use language conventions appropriately, especially punctuation and spelling, to aid meaning and presentation, and to enhance the reader's experience.

Student reflection note

Your teacher will provide a single page student reflection note for you to fill in and include with each text in your collection of texts. A sample student reflection note is included below:

Student reflection note	
School:	Student:
Title:	Genre:
I chose this genre because …	
My assessment of my work …	
What I learned from creating this text:	What I would do differently next time:
Teacher:	Date:

You will have time once the piece of writing is finished to think about what you learned and include it in the reflection note.

Features of quality

When the teacher is reading your work for the final assessment, he or she will choose one of the following **descriptors** to establish the **level of achievement** you have reached in your collection of written work.

Each piece of writing in your collection of work must have a student reflection note.

Features of quality for the collection of the student's texts
Exceptional – the student's text shows creativity and command of the chosen genre. The writing is highly competent, marked by original ideas, and imaginative word choices are perfectly suited to the purpose of the text. The work is fully shaped for its intended receiver/audience.
Above expectations – the student's text shows very good control of the chosen genre. The writing is consistently competent, and effective word choices are very well matched to the purpose of the text. The work is clearly shaped with the receiver/audience in mind.
In line with expectations – the student's text shows good awareness of the chosen genre. The writing is generally competent, and word choices match the purpose of the text well. Content and development of ideas reveal consistent awareness of the receiver/audience.
Yet to meet expectations – the student's text shows little awareness of the chosen genre. The writing lacks competence, and word choices may be inappropriate to the intended purpose of the text. Content and development of ideas reveal little awareness of a receiver/audience.

As you can see, each **descriptor identifies** a **standard** of focus, creativity, originality, technical skill and register. By dealing with your work in a focused way at all stages of the writing process, you will achieve a very high standard. The process of putting together the collection and selecting your best pieces means that you will be assessed only on your very highest-quality writing over the two years of Junior Cycle English. Crucially, it is your **personal choice** as to which pieces you submit.

Written assessment task

In the days and weeks following your submission of the collection of work, your class will be given a **written assessment task** to complete. The process will take place during two different classes:

During class 1: Stimulus and classroom discussion

Your teacher will show you a **short video clip** or play an audio extract where a **writer talks** about some **specific aspect of writing**.

It could be about why they wrote a certain piece, what **provoked or inspired** the writing. It might be about how they approach the **planning** of a piece of written work, or how useful **feedback** is in the process of **editing or re-drafting** work. It may also include discussion of aspects of the **genre** that writer works in: poetry, fiction, reporting, reviewing, etc.

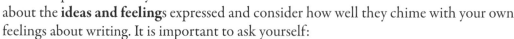

exam focus

The written assessment task takes place over two class periods: one class to view stimulus material, read the questions and discuss them, and one class to fill out your answers in the booklet.

Once you have viewed or listened to this **stimulus material** in class, your teacher will conduct a **discussion** about the points raised by the writer. You should think about the **ideas and feelings** expressed and consider how well they chime with your own feelings about writing. It is important to ask yourself:

1. Do I agree with the points made by this writer?
2. Why? Why not?
3. How would I respond if I was asked to answer the same questions?

Next, your teacher will discuss **prompts** or **areas of writing** that have been **discussed** in the **stimulus video/audio** and your class will discuss these prompts. The teacher will **distribute** a **booklet** of questions. This is your **written assessment task answer booklet.** You will be given time in class to **read and think** about the questions. As a class, you can **discuss the focus** of the questions and **how** you might begin to **approach answering** them. You will have **time** to **consider your answers** before writing.

L.O. R3

Use a wide range of reading comprehension strategies appropriate to texts, including digital texts:
- to retrieve information
- to link to previous knowledge
- to follow a process or argument
- to summarise, etc.

During class 2: Written assessment and submission

Your **teacher** will **distribute booklets** with the questions for your **written assessment**. You will also have **two texts you've created**, your **reflection notes** and any **previous draft material** relating to these texts **to refer** to, **examine** and **quote** from. There will be a **series of questions** which you have previously discussed in class. You will have **40 minutes** to complete your answers in the booklet.

When you are finished writing, you will **label** your booklet with your **exam number** and the teacher will collect them from the class. The booklets will be stored in the school and sent to SEC to be **corrected** with your **final exam** in June.

Only your **written assessment booklet** is sent to be corrected. The collection of work and reflection notes will be kept in the school and are not part of your final assessment.

Sample questions, answers and hints

Sections A & B   20 marks

Section A – Reflecting on a Text
Question 1

Give the titles of two texts, from your collection of texts, that you consider to be your best writing and identify the genre of each text.

First text:	*'Friday'*
Genre:	*Short story – opening paragraphs*
Second text:	*'Shylock's Diary'*
Genre:	*Diary extract*

Select an extract (for example, a paragraph, passage, or verse) from one text identified above. Copy the extract into the space provided below. The extract should not exceed 100 words .

> *I watched as he shook the iron key from the torn and battered envelope. It took him ages to open the front door. The place bore all the signs of its abandonment. Weeds sprouted from the gutters, cobwebs hung from the angle of each doorway.*
>
> *Inside, it smelled rotten and, sure enough, beneath the fanlight was the corpse of a robin.*
>
> *My companion spent a long time drifting between rooms, opening doors and sighing. On the sideboard in the drawing room he discarded his hat and the envelope bearing the solicitor's inscription 'To be presented to Mister Crusoe on his return from Polynesia.'*

First-person narrator ➤ I watched as he shook the iron key from the torn and battered envelope. It took **him** ages to open the front ◄ **Identity of character not revealed**
door. The place bore all the signs of its abandonment.
Detailed imagery ➤ Weeds sprouted from the gutters, cobwebs hung from the angle of each doorway.

Aesthetic use of language ➤ Inside, it smelled rotten and, sure enough, beneath the fanlight was the corpse of a robin.

Character suggested by actions ➤ My companion spent a long time drifting between rooms, opening doors and sighing. On the sideboard in the drawing room he discarded his hat and the envelope bearing the solicitor's inscription *'To be presented to Mister Crusoe on his return from Polynesia.'*

Hint

A sample **opening paragraph or paragraphs** from a **short story** are copied into the relevant space in the answer booklet. The **genre** is identified and several **typical features** of that genre are outlined. The annotated paragraph on the previous page demonstrates how the paragraph fulfils these criteria through the use of a first-person storyteller, creating a sense of mystery around the identity of characters, setting the scene with detailed images and appealing to the senses with aesthetic language.

Question 2

Write a response to either (a) or (b). Place a tick in the box next to your choice.

a) Explain how two features of the extract are typical of its genre.   ✓

b) Identify a change that you made in the course of writing this text that you think improved it and explain how it improved the text.

Hints

Write a short paragraph about how your story is a typical opening paragraph for a short story because it:

* Introduces the main character.
* Sets the scene well by giving detail or imagery.
* Hooks the reader by creating mystery/tension.
* Tells how the character feels by using a first-person narrator.

For each point, quote an example from your writing and explain briefly its relevance to the genre.

Read your reflection note again and think about the genre of your work and how you felt about drafting and editing your piece.

Sample answer

First text:	*'Friday'*
Genre:	*Short story – opening paragraphs*

My opening paragraph **sets the scene** in a way that is typical of a short story. The opening sentence establishes the voice of a **first-person narrator**. The reader will be curious about the identity of the narrator and also of his companion who is struggling 'to open the front door'.

Your teacher will allow 40 minutes for the written assignment to be completed.

Detailed images of a ruined building help to paint a clear picture of the setting, complete with sprouting 'weeds' and hanging 'cobwebs'. These visual clues help to establish the sense of a place which has been left empty for a long time.

In addition to the visual imagery, **aesthetic language** refers to the 'rotten' smell of the decaying 'robin'. By appealing to the reader's senses, the opening paragraphs create a deep awareness of the place where the story will unfold.

Finally, the personality of the companion is suggested by means of his sighing and 'drifting' between rooms. There is something mysterious and sad about this behaviour.

Section B – Reflecting on my Writing

Answer **two** of the following:

1. Where did my ideas come from?
2. Why is my second draft better than the first?
3. What did I learn about myself as a writer?
4. Ways I might use the skills I have learned.

key point

- Focus on the key words in the question, give evidence in the form of quotation and explain your points clearly.
- Illustrate the typical features of your chosen genre with examples from your **written piece of work.**

Hints

1. In preparation for the written assessment, think about the inspiration for your writing:
   - Was it based on a visual image, a story, TV show, advertisement, newspaper report or poem?
   - Is it a creative writing exercise written in response to the drama or fiction you have studied in your Junior Cycle English course?
   - Is it a fictional piece or does it contain elements of your own personal experience?
   - Did you collaborate with classmates in response to a title or question set by your teacher?

2. Your reflection should also include focused analysis of the differences between early versions of your writing and the finished product.
   - Did you delete lines or words? Why?
   - Were ideas suggested to you that allowed you to add to the passage to improve the quality?
   - How did you feel about making necessary changes?
   - Why is the final draft better than earlier versions?

3. Lessons you might have learned about yourself as a writer might include:
   - Genres I enjoy writing in most.
   - Influences on my imagination.
   - My writing style.
   - My feelings about editing and re-drafting work.

4. Areas where you might make good use of your writing and editing skills:
   - Collaborating with others to solve a problem.
   - Writing for pleasure to express myself.
   - Planning work to help provide a clear structure.
   - Coping with my feelings when I am given focused feedback about my work.

10 Basic Elements of Good Writing

In this section you will:
- Learn different **forms of sentences**.
- **Identify** essential **elements** of **good sentences**.
- Revise **paragraphing**, analysing well-written **sample paragraphs**.
- Explore a **variety of genres**: description, critical analysis, memoir and fiction.

Good writing is a **vital skill** for all students of English. This section will help you to **improve** your **writing** by **outlining** some **basic areas** of **grammar** and **spelling**.

In order to write well you must understand **how** to construct **proper sentences** and **paragraphs** and how to **avoid careless spelling mistakes**. This unit will revise these **basic elements** of **good writing**.

Sentences

Sentences are the **building blocks** of all writing. When we communicate clearly we are using words correctly to form sentences. Every sentence must have a **subject**, a **finite verb**, and make **complete sense**. A sentence can be a **statement**, **command** or **question**. Each sentence begins with a capital letter and ends with a **full stop, exclamation mark or question mark**.

Forms of sentences

1. **Subject:** The subject is **who or what** the sentence is **about**.
2. **Finite verb:** A finite verb is a verb which has a subject.
3. **Complete sense:** A group of words together **must make sense** in order to function as a sentence.

> **Rome is the capital city of Italy.**

The **subject** here is 'Rome', the **finite verb** is the verb to be ('is'), and no additional words or phrases are needed for the sentence to **make sense**. This sentence is a **statement**. Most of your writing is composed of statements.

> ## Is Rome the capital of Italy?

The **subject** is still 'Rome' and **verb** is still to be ('Is'). These six words together have a **clear meaning**. This time the sentence is a **question**. Always add a **question mark** to the end of a question.

> ## Fly to Rome immediately!

In this sentence the **subject is implied**, but the reader understands that a word such as 'you' has been left out to convey a sense of urgency. The **verb** 'Fly' is in the imperative mood and the four words together form a **coherent command**.

Types of sentences

There are four types of sentences:

1. **Simple**
2. **Double**
3. **Multiple**
4. **Complex**

1. Sentences are <u>simple</u> if there is only **one finite verb**:

> ## Today is Saturday.

2. A <u>double sentence</u> consists of **two simple sentences joined by a conjunction**. There must be **two finite verbs**:

> ## Put on your coat and leave at once!

Each of the simple sentences that together form this double sentence is a **main clause**. This means that the **clause makes sense on its own**, e.g. *'Leave at once.'*

3. A <u>multiple sentence</u> will combine **several main clauses** to produce a long sentence:

> ## He shot the sheriff, the heroine fainted and the curtain fell.

Use double and multiple sentences to give **variety** to your writing style.

4. A <u>complex sentence</u> is composed of a **main clause** and one or more **subordinate clauses**:

> ## Once you have poured the wine, you may serve the starters.

The **main clause** in this sentence is *'You may serve the starters.'*
The subordinate clause **depends on** the main clause for its meaning and here the **subordinate clause** is *'Once you have poured the wine.'*

Conjunctions are the words used to **join up** or **link** the **main clause and the subordinate clause**:

after	although	as	before	besides
how	since	so	though	once
until	when	where	while	unless

Everything you write relies on sentences. If your sentences are correctly written then the reader will understand what you have written. While sentences are the basic units of language, paragraphs are about developing those ideas, explaining, illustrating or expanding them at length.

L.O. R 11

Identify and comment on features of English at word and sentence level using appropriate terminology, showing how such features contribute to overall effect.

Paragraphs

A **paragraph** is a **group of sentences** with a **united purpose**. All the sentences in a paragraph are linked by a **common idea**, theme or concept. When you have explored or developed one idea and are ready to move on to the next, you must begin with a **new paragraph**. This is essential to give your reader a sense of the **logical organisation** of your written work. Good paragraphing helps the reader to have a **clear idea** of the **shape** and purpose the piece.

When you **plan** well, it helps to give you an image of the overall arrangement of your paragraphs. At the planning stage you should also think about how you will link or connect one paragraph to the next.

The paragraph usually begins with a **key sentence** from which all the other sentences flow. **Key sentences** establish an idea and the **subsequent sentences** in a paragraph **develop, expand, explain or illustrate** these initial ideas.

Look carefully at the following three paragraphs taken from the travel book *In Patagonia*, written by English travel writer Bruce Chatwin.

> A Boer gave me a lift back south, through Perito Moreno, to Arroyo Feo, where the volcanic badlands began. He was a veterinary surgeon and he didn't think much of the other Boers.

> A frill of pleated white cliffs danced round the horizon. The surface of the ground was blotched with scabs of dribbling magenta. I spent the night with a road gang, whose caravans sat inside a ring of yellow bulldozers. The men were eating greasy fritters and asked me to share them. Perón smirked over the company.

> Among them was a Scot with ginger hair and the physique of a caber thrower. He peered at me with milky blue eyes, feeling out affinities of race and background with a mixture of curiosity and pain. His name was Robbie Ross.

The **first paragraph** deals with **identifying the motorist** who brought Chatwin to a place called Arroyo Feo. It only contains two sentences, the second of which gives more **detail** about the man, his **occupation** and his **dislike for his countrymen**.

Once this writer changes to **describing a place** he begins a **new paragraph**. All five sentences in the second paragraph are linked because they give us **information** about the **landscape** of Arroyo Feo or tell us about **what happened** on the night in question.

There is a change to another **new paragraph** when the writer begins to discuss one **unusual character** called Robbie Ross. Every time you introduce a **change of character, event, time or location** you must begin a **new paragraph**. All genres require this basic logical approach to paragraphing.

Descriptive paragraphs

In the paragraph below, the writer Joe O'Connor is describing a disco he used to attend as a teenager.

> It used to be the last song of the night at the Presentation College disco, Glasthule, where I first strutted my funky stuff. 'Prez', as it was known, was a pretty rough joint. They searched you outside for strong drink and offensive weapons and if you didn't have any, they didn't let you in. But 'Stairway to Heaven' reduced even the most hardened knackers, savage boot boys and nefarious ne'er-do-wells to wide-eyed blubbing wrecks. I can still see it now, a great head-banging mass of denim and cheesecloth and existential angst.

The **initial sentence identifies** the disco and all the **other sentences** in the paragraph help that sentence by giving more precise **detail**. If you are writing a memoir-style piece where you are discussing aspects of your own experience, then you should **illustrate your points well** by giving clear and accurate **examples**.

> ➡️ **L.O. R 9**
>
> Identify, appreciate and compare the ways in which different literary, digital and visual genres and sub-genres shape texts and shape the reader's experience of them.

Discursive paragraphs

The **most common verb** used in all examination papers is the word **'discuss'**. If you check this verb in a thesaurus, the list of similar words you find helps to illustrate **what you are expected to do** when you are asked to **'discuss'** a topic. **'Talk about', 'explain', 'analyse'** and **'consider'** are all useful alternative ways to outline the **purpose of 'discussing'** in an exam answer. What do all of these tasks have in common? **Outlining your ideas** and **giving reasons** to **back up** those **opinions**. This is the type of writing that is most essential for performing well in most written exams. Look closely at the **sample question** on the following page from a Junior Cycle English exam paper.

Read the sample answer, discussing or **analysing** the **visual impact** of the poster. Then practise by attempting to write your own **discursive paragraph** in answer to the second part of the question.

Sample question and answer

Question 1   10 marks

Write a **critical analysis** of the poster of *Fantastic Beasts & Where to Find Them*, featured on the Junior Cycle Exam 2017. In it you should consider the visual impact of the poster.

Allow 6 minutes for 10-mark questions.

> For copyright reasons the publisher is unable to reproduce this image. The complete paper is available for download on the State Examination Commission website www.examinations.ie.

Sample answer – critical analysis

The **visual impact** of this movie poster is based on two elements:

The **graphic** is made up of several parts. The **background shows** medieval buildings in a mountainous location. They appear almost in **silhouette** on the skyline. Above them are two flying creatures. They seem to be **mythological hybrid beasts**. To the **centre right** of the image we see three dogs' heads.

The final **graphic element** is the **human figure** dominating the poster. He is dressed in black, holding a lighted staff in his right hand. His eyes are in the **shade** but visible enough for us to see his serious expression. All of these elements are familiar as **settings** and **characters** reminiscent of the *Harry Potter* franchise of books, movies and games.

Always write in black pen and only on ruled lines of your answer booklet. Any additional paragraphs in longer answers should be clearly labelled on the first line of a new ruled page.

Secondly, **verbal details** in the poster also contribute to its **visual impact**. Across the top of the poster, a **banner** proclaims, 'From the author of The Harry Potter Saga'. This **anchors** the meaning of the image, communicating ideas about **genre, character** and **mood**. In **reversed-out print** at the bottom of the image we read the name of the **protagonist** 'Newt Scamander' and the **title** of the movie *Fantastic Beasts & Where to Find Them*. Clearly the creatures in the **background** are the 'Fantastic Beasts'. All of the **copy** is printed in an archaic **font**, suggesting an old tale set in the historical past. Finally, the familiar shield **logo** of Warner Brothers is placed in white against a black background in the bottom-right corner of the image. This is also a **visual link** to the well-known *Harry Potter* series.

Autobiographical paragraphs

Personal writing implies that the subject matter and style of your writing in this question should be drawn from **your own experience and opinions**. Autobiographical or **memoir**-style writing should draw material from **your own direct experience**. The following paragraph illustrates this point. It is taken from *Pictures in My Head,* the memoir of the Irish film star Gabriel Byrne. In this paragraph, Gabriel recreates the **detail** and **sensations** of his **first trip to the cinema** in the company of his granny. Notice how well this **paragraph illustrates** this **experience** by reference to aspects of **colour and movement.**

> All around the foyer there were painted photographs of men with black moustaches and women with bright red lipstick like my mother. Then the sentry pulled back the door and we were in darkness with the noise of those strange voices all around us. We edged our way along by a wall like blind people, me holding on to her coat for fear, till suddenly in an explosion of blinding colour, I saw before me the bluest sea I could ever imagine, and on it two huge boats with sails, sailing under a vast blueness of sky. I turned my head in terror into her body, and for an eternity of moments I dared not look again. When I opened my eyes I saw a light beam in the darkness and a voice asked for our tickets, as it came toward us. And with her arm around me, we followed the dancing light as it lit our way along the steps, 'til we found our seats and I sat down overwhelmed by the fear and the mystery and the magic of it all. But as the wonder grew, the terror died. And so I came to know the lovely dark womb of the picture-house for the first time.

This paragraph deals with the **topic** of the writer's memory of a **key moment from his childhood**. The whole paragraph is a **development** of the experience of moving through the foyer and into the dark interior of the picture house. Byrne captures the excitement through his attention to the **details** of **sensation and emotion**. A relatively brief incident is slowed down for the reader and we are treated to a **well-illustrated account** of what was happening, **what he saw** and what he **heard and felt**. Ultimately, the last sentence gives us a curious **image**, the **metaphor** of the cinema as a 'womb' suggesting comfort and security, but also hinting that this was where his desire to act was formed and developed.

Narrative paragraphs

You will need to be very careful about the paragraphs of a short story. The rule is quite simple: change to a **new paragraph** every time you switch to a **new location, time, event, or character**. Every **new line of dialogue** should begin a **new paragraph**.

The episode below is taken from a short story called 'Snot's Green Sea' by Frances Cotter. Notice that the extract is made up of **nine separate paragraphs**.

> After the MP3 incident, I was more tuned into Snot. (That's nearly a joke … I think … tuned in … like on a radio … except it's an MP3 player.) I was really keen to know what was on the machine.
>
> Once, in the dressing room, I saw his jacket and slipped my hand in his pocket. I felt the cool, rectangular shape and the two thin leads. I rummaged for the switch and was just about to turn it on, when BANG!
>
> I was on the ground. My ear was bursting as if it was filled with hot chilli sauce. For a second I thought the earplug was a booby trap like a 007 device, but then I saw Snot's white knuckles.
>
> 'Don't you ever touch my stuff. Do you hear?'
>
> 'But Snot, I just wanted to –'
>
> 'It's none of your business!'
>
> His face was very near mine.
>
> 'Okay Snot, I was just wondering … I won't – '
>
> I was on my feet and running.

The **short paragraphs** are merited here for several reasons. First of all, the **change** to the dressing room requires a **new paragraph**. Next, there is the paragraph where the **central character** on the ground is recovering from a blow to the head. Each **line of dialogue** is given a **new paragraph** to help the reader to follow the story and realise which of the two characters is speaking. The final line is a **new paragraph** because a **new action** or event is happening.

 L.O. W 10

Use and apply knowledge of language structures, for example
- sentence structure
- paragraphing
- grammar

to make writing a richer experience.

Short sentences and **paragraphs** are appropriate here, as the **quick pace** of writing enhances the **drama** of this episode.

If you are writing a **short story** then it should include **dialogue**. Do not include too much dialogue – a good writer will use reported speech sparingly. Choose a key moment in the story to have characters speak aloud to each other. The exchange of spoken words should be important. Remember: you do not need to have the characters say everything, often we communicate as much by what is left unsaid.

Spelling

Many students lose marks because of poor spelling. You can **improve your overall grade** by spending time learning to **spell correctly**. The following is a list of **frequently occurring words** that are often misspelt. Learn to spell each word correctly and check the meaning in a dictionary.

absolutely	because	completely	ecstasy	government
accept	beginning	concentrate	efficient	grateful
accidentally	believe	conscious	embarrassment	guarantee
achieve	benefit	courageous	emergency	guard
across	between	criticism	emphasise	happened
address	bicycle	deceive	enough	happiness
although	biscuit	decision	equipment	haven't
always	breathe	definitely	essential	hear
anxious	brilliant	descend	every	height
apologise	brought	describe	exaggerate	heroes
appearance	business	desperate	excellent	hospital
argument	category	development	excitement	humour
around	caught	different	exhausted	hypocrisy
arrange	certain	disappear	experience	illustrate
ascend	character	disappointing	extremely	imagination
association	choose	disaster	fascinating	immediately
awful	clothes	discuss	fierce	important
awkward	college	disease	foreign	independent
background	coming	doesn't	friends	influence
beautiful	committed	dropped	fulfilled	intelligence

interesting	morning	possession	right	thought
irrelevant	mysterious	practice	schedule	together
knew	necessary	prejudice	scene	tragedy
knight	nervous	present	science	tragic
knowledge	night	privilege	secretary	tranquil
laugh	nothing	purpose	sense	truly
leave	nuisance	queue	separate	unconscious
leisure	occasion	read	should	unnecessary
library	occurred	realise	similar	until
licence	office	really	since	using
light	once	receipt	sincerely	usually
literature	only	received	skilful	valuable
loneliness	opinion	recognise	solemn	vengeance
lonely	organise	recommend	something	vicious
loose	original	reference	sometimes	view
magazine	panicked	reign	sound	village
maintenance	parallel	relief	started	weird
making	parliament	religion	still	which
marriage	particularly	repetition	stopped	while
meant	permanent	responsible	straight	whole
medicine	physical	restaurant	strategy	whose
medieval	pleasant	rhyme	success	would
might	please	rhythm	surprise	write
minutes	poem	ridiculous	sympathy	

More spellings

The words given below include **homophones** – words that sound the same but have different meanings – as well as other pairs of words often used incorrectly in student writing, e.g. 'I would of ...' should be 'I would have ...'

Learn how to **spell them**, check the **meaning** of each word, and write a sentence for each word, using it **correctly**.

allowed/aloud	its/it's	sight/site	weak/week
bear/bare	lone/loan	steel/steal	weather/
fare/fair	of/off/have	tail/tale	whether
for/four	one/won	their/there/they're	we're/were
groan/grown	pain/pane	thought/taught	wear/where
here/hear	past/passed	through/threw	weight/wait
higher/hire	piece/peace	to/two/too	whose/who's
hole/whole	plane/plain	vain/vein	write/right
hour/our	purpose/propose	warn/worn	your/you're
idol/idle	quiet/quite	waste/waist	

Acknowledgements

The author and publisher are grateful to the following for permission to reproduce copyrighted material:

Reckless: The Petrified Flesh reproduced by kind permission of the author, Cornelia Funke and her team at Breathing Books.

Extract from Carriehopefletcher.com reproduced by kind permission of the author, Carrie Hope Fletcher.

Crown of Midnight by Sarah J. Maas. Copyright © Sarah J. Maas, 2013, *Crown of Midnight*, Bloomsbury Publishing Inc.

Mountains of the Mind: A History of a Fascination by Robert MacFarlane. Copyright © Robert MacFarlane, 2003, Granta Books.

'Blessing' by Imtiaz Dharker. Copyright © Imtiaz Dharker, *Postcards from God* (Bloodaxe Books, 1997). Reproduced with permission of Bloodaxe Books.

'Driving Home at Dusk with Donal, 4' by Don Byrne from *Soft Shoes and Sunshine*, Summer Palace Books (2004).

'In Memory of George Best' is from *That Which is Suddenly Precious: Poems 1975–2015* by Dermot Bolger, published by New Island Books and is reprinted by permission of the author.

Private Peaceful © Michael Morpurgo adapted by Simon Reade, 2013. By kind permission of Oberon Books Ltd.

Making a Difference by Padraic Mullen. Reproduced by kind permission of the author, Padraic Mullen.

Letter to my 8-year-old self by Jim Kirby. Reproduced by kind permission of the author, Jim Kirby.

'La La Land review: You'll fall in love with the movies again. 5 stars' by Rohan Naahar, Hindustan Times, 2017. Reproduced by kind permission of the author, Rohan Naahar.

'Digging', 'Mid-term Break', 'Lovers on Aran' from *Death of a Naturalist* by Seamus Heaney, published by Faber and Faber Ltd. Copyright © Seamus Heaney, 1966.

'Base Details' by Siegfried Sassoon. Copyright © Siegfried Sassoon by kind permission of the Estate of George Sassoon.

From *To Kill A Mockingbird* by Harper Lee, published by William Heinemann. Reprinted by permission of The Random House Group Limited. © 1960.

'The Man' speech from *School of Rock,* directed by Richard Linklater. Copyright © Richard Linklater, Paramount Pictures, 2003.

The Peregrine by J.A Baker. Copyright © J.A Baker, 1967.

'The Outing' from *Can't and Won't* by Lydia Davis. Copyright © Lydia Davis, 2014.

Artemis Fowl by Eoin Colfer. Copyright © Eoin Colfer, 2001.

Of Mice and Men by John Steinbeck. Copyright © John Steinbeck, 1937.

'Phenomenal Woman' from *And Still I Rise* by Maya Angelou. Copyright © Maya Angelou, 1978.

'Stopping by Woods on a Snowy Evening' from *Collected Poems* by Robert Frost. Copyright © Robert Frost, 1930.

'Miracle on St. David's Day' from *Collected Poems 2008* by Gillian Clarke. Copyright © Gillian Clarke, Carcanet Press, 2008.

'The Ring' from *The End of the World & Other Stories* by Bryan MacMahon. Copyright © Bryan MacMahon, 1976, by permission of A.P Watt Ltd.

'A Child Half Asleep' from *Tony Connor: New and Selected Poems 1982* by Tony Connor. Copyright © Tony Connor, Carcanet Press, 1982.

The authors and publisher have made every effort to trace all copyright holders, but if any has been inadvertently overlooked we would be pleased to make the necessary arrangement at the first opportunity.